My Life in England
Dream Come True or Ruin?

by
Ms. Ntsoaki Mary Mosoeunyane

DORRANCE
PUBLISHING CO
EST. 1920
PITTSBURGH, PENNSYLVANIA 15238

Dorrance Publishing Co
585 Alpha Drive
Suite 103
Pittsburgh, PA 15238
Visit our website at www.dorrancebookstore.com

ISBN: 978-1-4809-1017-1
eISBN 978-1-4809-1339-4

TABLE OF CONTENTS

Acknowledgements

A man is not an island. Indeed without support, I would not have been inspired to write. When the idea of writing for publication came to mind, I talked about it to friends, family, acquaintances, etc. It was an attempt to make the idea come alive so I could have the strength to carry out the project. I therefore thank every person who helped keep me focused on my dream. It is from my accumulated experiences and talks with people that this book was born.

I'd like to thank in a special way my friends from near and far who helped shape my thoughts, read my work, and gave me honest constructive criticism about how I have written. Some took special time off from their schedules to proofread. My mother, my hero, has contributed to everything I am. My children, my strength, asked probing questions about the book and its completion, so they could read it and take it to school. To every person who encouraged me in one form or another, and lastly to you, the reader, for spending your money to buy the book and telling others about it, thank you.

Introduction

This is a real story of experiences gained in my life so far. As a child, I always liked to write daily about everything that happened in my life (I still keep a journal today). In fact, my book was born out of writing a journal. When my life lacked depth, I put pen to paper. I used it as escape, logging my thoughts as I looked for the meaning in my life. I have kept diaries and journals most of my life, writing anything that came to mind or happened. I wrote down what made me happy and unhappy. I loved writing, but I never thought of myself as a professional writer. If someone had channelled my skill in the right direction I would by now have written volumes. I wrote to my friends far and near. I even enjoyed pen friends or simply sharing writings with one childhood friend. He liked writing, and we used to write our thoughts, experiences, and share them. He was quite poetic, and so I am not surprised he is one of the country's prime literature teachers and scriptwriters today. I wish I kept the letters we wrote, because they were full of fun and giggles. We would write about the boys and girls we each had come across, life in its depth, and more. I have yet to see his work as we lost contact at the time when he was writing something for publication.

This book is not written in any particular style. It was written as I received inspiration from life and is organized into chapters to give it structure.

My friends thought I had a very interesting approach to life. When we were in college they used to sneak and read my diary behind my back. I once caught them giggling away in the room I shared with one of them as they went through the pages of my diary. I think they found it amusing that I wrote everything I felt and experienced daily, and this helped to fill their empty days. When they saw me, they just laughed more. They knew that I was naïve and that there wouldn't be any scary stuff in my writing. Later, when we moved to another city, I read my roommate's diary, and I swore that day I would never read anyone's diary no matter how close or carefree we were with each other. She never knew that I read her diary. I was crippled with fear as the diary taught me that she was in serious trouble that she never shared with me. I could not approach her as it was really personal. All I did was pray for her and hope for the best. If she reads the book, I will confess.

This book is my life as I have lived it and the experiences of other people that have shaped who I am today. It is our book, those of us that share its sentiments. I have always romanticized and made scripts of life and love in my mind. My friends always called me a hopeless romantic; maybe my first book should have been a love story. Most of my thoughts went down on paper and just became well-kept stories that never reached other people. Why then do I want to publish now? Because of the experiences I have had in the short span of time while living in England, the reality of life there, rather than what I had expected. This has made me want to tell a story which needs to be told. It won't be about what has happened in England only, as you can appreciate that my life began long before the move to England. But the experience in England has created a desire to share it with the world. I am not just telling a story. I aim to enlighten and encourage similar writings from others, hoping that as a collective, we may impact change in society. I am writing to a wide audience—all those who love to read real-life stories!

It's dedicated to my mum, a single parent, and my late dad, whose life and love shaped our own lives—his love for my mum was a testament to true love. And to my two lovely children whose trying energy keeps me alive. And to every person I know who has touched my heart in one form or another. I have really been blessed in my life to meet people who are lovely. I believe being in favour with God earns you favour with other people, but I am not implying that God has favourites. Read on!

As this is based on my life, I will take you on a journey of experiencing life as I have lived it, sharing observations I have made about different things, and perceiving them as I have. I will share some insights from one stage or another from my walk and share various strategies to create a fulfilled you amidst challenges of racial discrimination and life's general pressures. My dream is to write, to be successful at it, and also to encourage my people to share their heritage in writing. There is a writer in most of us! I would love to expand more on education about prejudice and living without it for a better world! I love real-life stories, so I hope to publish more of them. My next book will be along the lines of living in harmony in a multicultural society—an educational piece in accepting diversity. After all, variety is the spice of life. I had thought of The Break Up: When Does It Begin, as the next book to write. But now I strongly believe a follow-up book that will address how to move forward from shared experiences as more appropriate. Thanks for the feedback from various publishers for appropriateness of a follow-up book to keep the idea alive. My dream is to have a full, established curriculum within schools on matters of prejudice and how not to fall victim to it. People try to put others in a box due to their lack of knowledge or understanding of the negative impact of social isolation based on racial prejudice. I believe, if we teach the children who will make up society later, we will be in a better position to get rid of prejudice. We can then truly claim we are a civilised society!

Chapter One
Beginnings

My ambition to explore the western world began as I boarded that plane to England in search of a dream! It landed at London Heathrow on a chilly February morning in 2000. The land looked grey and sad with no greenery. I am not sure about being excited, but I knew that this marked yet another beginning for me. I settled into life and got married a year and half later. I have two wonderful children who are now eleven and nine years old. I was born in Lesotho, the beautiful "Mountain Kingdom in the sky," to two wonderful parents. Lesotho is a small country that is totally surrounded by South Africa (SA), thus our economy is dependent on South Africa. Lesotho is a very mountainous place with the most amazing landscapes known! It is one of the poor countries of the world with a population of just about two million (www.indexmundi.com, 2012). It is just over thirty thousand square kilometres in size. You would think, with such a population, we would be living comfortably or at least with no one hungry for basic needs. If the leaders actually loved the country and its people, the Basotho, we would be living with a narrow gap between the poor and the rich. But those who should lead the country properly and serve its people (who voted them into these positions) are busy investing in themselves at the expense of the wider population. They live in big houses with bodyguards and so on and send their kids to expensive schools out of the country where there's a stronger economy, using the taxpayers' money to educate their children at the higher cost.

Lesotho is indeed an amazingly beautiful country and rich in some resources that should be channelled rightly. One of the resources we possess is water, which could be used to generate enough electricity to supply the whole country. But the leaders let other countries take over these kind of projects, getting close to nothing in return as these money cannot be accounted for by the authority running the project.

The population has diminished due to poverty, lack of food, subjecting people to all sorts of ailments, and infections (with HIV sweeping the nation in the last decade). People have a shorter life span due to generally poor nutrition (to the advantage of the virus) and other opportunistic infections. Poverty rates are also high as the land becomes barren due to serious soil erosion that makes it impossible to grow much from the land. The discrepancy between the poor and the rich is vast. Most poor people remain poor with literally nothing to eat, surviving on donations from other people or nations. You go around the country, and it's sad to realise that the boy who has been a shepherd will remain a shepherd into adult life. There are no other strategies of improving such lives.

The architecture of the country is another factor. The highly mountainous slopes cause crops to be washed away with the soil during the rainy season. Poor farming practices due to lack of resources is another factor. The educated are mostly the ones who make a better life. Not everyone has a chance to receive an education, which is a shame as there are so many children with extreme potential who are just left behind. If I could change anything in my country, it would be a recommendation for free education through and through. I have learned that in 2000 there was a plan for a free primary education. But this was only implemented in 2006. My question though is what then happens after primary education, which is only up to seven years? This will enable children to read and write, but those whose parents cannot afford secondary school fees will not make it to college and university. Is the country really solving long-term problems? We can clearly say no! However, there are ongoing initiatives for better education for the Basotho. In comparison, more women are literate compared to the male counterpart—men have to think of providing for their families quite early in life. Lesotho, interestingly, has a generally higher literacy rate compared to other African countries (www.indexmundi.com, 2012).

It is also rather unfortunate that a lot of talent in manual skills have no outlet. I reflect on days of growing up when boys use to make cars with wires as lovely toys that kids pushed around the streets. But in the business market you will not see any of these being sold by local stores as no one creates that vision in the society. Some of them could even win prices at exhibitions, etc. Who will create space for such developments? Everyone believes in formal education, yet not everybody has an opportunity to get there. There is a lot to be done—you may say who will do it when every potential person (including me) is leaving the country? The outside exposure is good as well, because it changes your perspective. Had I not left Lesotho, I would probably not have a stronger vision of what could be! I would be enjoying the comfort of those in my class who won't go hungry. People tend to get comfortable and used to their lifestyle, forgetting collective success.

Despite all the other downfalls, Lesotho is an amazingly beautiful country with lots of tourist attractions: Katse dam, water falls, skiing mountains, national parks, etc. In the small village where my father was born, they built a Basotho hut with a thatched roof. Well, not out of pride, but among the African huts, the Basotho have the neatest form (google "Basotho village" for proof). This kind of housing is very cool; it is made of stones, sticks, or mud. Typically those that stand out are built of stone. I do not remember so much of my life then, but I have always cherished the moments when I visited my village.

The village was in a valley, surrounded by mountains, a stream running through it, and the river (Orange River) running parallel to the village. It served as a border between the other villages. Thinking about it, it was set up in the most beautiful location where you could hear the birds singing and the water from the steams making the most amazing sounds ever. Today, it could be a perfect location for a perfect holiday, something like the little Greek islands, a nice get away from busy city lives! This place is more than that. I still have to take my children to see this place, but from a distance, as the village does not exist anymore. Who knows, I might be lucky and build a dream holiday resort in this location, a tribute to my father. In those days, the Basotho rated certain houses for urban living only. There was a myth that in a village the first man to build an urban house usually dies. Immediately following their marriage, my father built his own house as he understood he now had his own family. He was the first man to build what was considered an urban (mabalane) house in that village. My father died as I mentioned, but as for the myth, people believe what makes sense to them. In fact he was the first in that village to die so young before his father (he was only thirty-two years old). Yes, they got married young, as my mum was twenty-eight at this time. Thinking about it, most people today get married very late as they pursue a career first before marriage and children. My parents channelled me toward education so I did exactly that. There is a saying in Sesotho "Sejana se setle ha se jele", meaning good people often die of unfortunate circumstances.

Everyone knew my father was a good, successful man, who was willing to share his skills with the village as a form of empowerment. Success did not make him inhumane. In fact, my father seemed to have understood that success is not measured by individual achievements, but by the community at large. He built the community by organizing skill-development strategies and social committees for entertainment. They were a great team, him with my mother, as they arranged food for these gatherings and mokete (feast), where people gather together for fun and share ideas of community building. These gatherings also helped to unite the community. My father worked away from home for the majority of the time, but whenever he came home, he and my mum were busy organising the community for one thing or the other. I learned like any other child that as a child you belong to the community. You look up to all the adults for guidance. You would not get away with mischief in the absence of your parents as every adult was responsible for disciplining any child who was involved in any form of mischief. People simply looked out for each other in unity. Reflecting on this, my kids are growing up in a very different environment where even I have to try hard to adjust, an environment where you should not dare open your mouth trying to reprimand someone's child despite your intentions. Unfortunately, it is the same even for those belonging to a small, church family.

So you can appreciate that even though I am an only child, I have never felt isolated by relatives or my community at large. I am told that the attitudes of people are changing as people adapt to a more city-centric life like anywhere else in the world. Talking to the older generation in the UK, gave me the insight that at some stage, they were also community orientated and not so individualistic like today.

Unfortunately, my mum explained to me, our wonder village had to be eradicated. When my grandfather died, greedy people from near and far came and stole every animal he owned. He was not a king or chief, but he had an authority that people feared or respected, so this was their chance. My grandfather had power over others, because he was the richest man of the village. He owned every animal for farming, the selling of mohair, domestic use, and transport (horses), etc. A lot of his possessions came from my father's hard work from an early age prior his marriage to my mother. My father had success written all over him as he was channelled, focused, had a purpose, and knew what he wanted out of life— though his was short lived .

In my memory and from what I learned from my mum, I had a wonderful childhood, the kind in which I belonged to a huge family and society at large. Children belonged to their parents and also were the responsibility of all adults in the community. So though I was an only child, I don't remember being alone. The society was close-knit, and people looked out for each other. Thinking back, that was a good way of life (as long as people did not get into your business too much). I grew up in an environment that was protective and loving. My family—aunties, uncles, cousins, etc.—were all protective of me. My mother, whom we, my family and friends, all called "Tetas," brought me up as a single parent. My father, who was simply the perfect (not meaning without fault) husband and great father, died when I was just nine years old. My mum often says, "If he had been ill, I would accept it better." This is indeed the painful part, as he was murdered by two of his colleagues out of jealousy. They plotted his murder.

You see, my father was a very intelligent black man, a strong, tall, and extremely handsome hunk. I see traces of him in my son. Interest-

4

ingly, my daughter resembles my mum. In Africa, there are different ethnic groups within the black people. Because of the politics of ethnicity in South Africa, these guys were resistant of my father's position over them. He worked in the mining industry, and being a Mosotho from Lesotho, in their understanding, they should have gotten his position. Most men from Lesotho in my father's time worked in the mining industries in SA or Gauteng as it is still called (meaning gold), due to the lack of local resources and job provision. You have different skill mixes (the labourers usually went right underground). My father was lucky to hold the position he had even though he did not have a prior education or training for it. He was naturally intelligent, so he was easily educated and obtained managerial skills. He therefore held a management position where he led a group of men in accomplishing various tasks.

As physically strong and fit as my father was, he was the nicest guy you could come across. He would never harm a soul. But if you crossed his path, he would deal with you as a man. So his assassins knew they stood no chance of approaching him face to face. They then began their evil plot, which cost his life. The report revealed they stabbed him three times on the chest near his heart. He lost strength from severe bleeding and help came too late. My family was told that the two men who stabbed him to death worked under his supervision. They intentionally resisted their duty to carry out tasks as assigned as a way of showing they did not want him to hold that position. In their low minds, as natives of SA, they deserved preference of such positions whether or not they were qualified or merited it.

When I think about it, it especially saddens me knowing that justice was not carried out. In those days, my mum did not know how to follow up the case any better so the guilty could be brought to justice. All my family received from SA was a dead body and reports of how he died. A friend whose father (an Afrikaner or Boer) worked at around the time of my father in the industry said her father would be willing to assist me even today if I wanted to find out who were the killers of my father. It would bring some closure, I guess, but I am not sure I want to go through that. Some people even speculate that maybe someone else was behind it—the white South Africans. I never bought into this one. To begin with, they gave him the position. Also, I have only been racially aware now as an adult. I do reflect on it, thinking that if the same guys are alive today, they are grandfathers while my children have been deprived of such an opportunity. Unfortunately, even their father's dad is deceased. My mother has not really gotten over his death or the circumstances surrounding it. She was scared to marry again, probably fearing the unpredictable. Well, there are many issues around it.

If you think discrimination is about black versus white, then think again. In the thick of apartheid in SA, blacks being discriminated upon by whites, the black people would stop at nothing to discriminate against other blacks that weren't South African. What a sad world. I look at my children and feel sad that they will grow up never experiencing the touch, love, and strength inherent in my father. I was also deprived of having such a man to look up to for strength. Besides my own memories of my father, my mum has done a good job of teaching me his nature. I used to fantasize about marrying a man like my father—did I? I guess the fact that we are not together explains it.

This movement of men working in SA promoted some community unity among women whose husbands spent months away from home. It was a system where men left their homes for about three months at a time to work and provide for the family's needs. So, when your father came home, everyone in the village was happy as it provided an opportunity for kids to get some goodies. I recall vividly that when my father came home one holiday, all the children came over for goodies. It was a norm for the society to include others in your joy. It was in my father's nature to provide and share anyway. I do not recall any excitement of getting goodies from other fathers after my fathers' death or while he was alive. He was the life of the community, and so without him everyone kind of lost that vibrancy of life. Thinking about it, my grandfather in seeking a good land for grazing and crop planting had moved away from his family (the brothers, uncles, sisters, etc.), so the people who lived in our village were mostly from around our glen and looked up to our family for support.

As I grew older, I began to understand some of the reasons my mother never remarried. She did everything to protect me. You see, I was very jealous whenever any male spoke to her. It did not matter the relationship they had or whether they used to visit or talk to her even during my father's life. I used to be crippled with the fear that maybe they would take her away from me and I would end up with no parents. It is funny, and we talk about it today. She says she was scared also that the emotional trauma I would face might be too damaging and that would destroy her. You have to understand that I was very precious in their eyes as an only child. When my mum lost my brother who was born prematurely due to medical problems, my father vowed that there would be no other children after me; he would not take the chance of losing my mother as well. She was very unwell throughout the pregnancy and nearly lost her life. For an African man of my father's time, it was very unusual for a man to opt out of having children to save his wife. But he was different, and my mum knew it. If I were still naive, I would say he had a Western mentality. But I have now learned and seen that people are people regardless of where they come from. There is this ideology that if one marries a white man, they will have the best, free life. The Western way of thinking will be reflected upon in many chapters of this book. Human beings are human beings at the end of the day, with only slight differences here and there.

When older and wiser, I told my mum that she could get married. I was no longer jealous. She just laughed it off every time and said that she wouldn't fit into that life anymore. Well, she just turned sixty in April of 2010. So technically she has many years ahead if God lends her breath of life. But I think she is so used to her life now, it would bring a lot of readjustments if she got married. In a way, in my country, it is still a taboo to get married at that age.

People are funny creatures; they smile but bite your back when you are not looking. As much as my father was loved by people for his goodness, at the time when he died, at the freshness of emotional trauma, cruel spiteful words were heard from some people. They wondered whether my mum would still afford the fine things of life, if she would manage my school fees or the small shop they had, etc. Naively, I would pass these comments to my mother with the names of the people. I did not realize the damaging power of such words. But my mum never made anything out of it. She would say they were the losers— now that's strength! And indeed this is what I know of my mum, a builder and not a destroyer.

My father was the sole breadwinner by choice. My father was a hard worker, community builder, and a family man. He wanted the best for us, and for those times in that village, he was the ideology of success. Within that village we had a better life than most. In the months preceding his death, he had gently urged my mother to get a job as life is unpredictable. He went on and on about how he wouldn't want me to end up with no education because she could not afford to pay the fees. On this, they were in accord. My mum had always worked hard, so she took well to getting a job (they were a good team in working hard).

You know how we often say that some people can sense their death. My father, as we reviewed events prior to his death, was preparing my mum for the worst-case scenario. My mum took a job since that time. She did different jobs in shops, restaurants, and got her business ideas as she worked her life away to support me as well as her family. Unlike my father, my mum's family were poor and did not own much. I used to cry sometimes when my mum would tell me about some of her experiences growing up. How my grandmother suffered to put food on the table for all eight children. My grandfather (her father) was an extremely lazy man who did nothing to support them. But like a good woman, my grandmother toiled to ensure her children survived. In fact it was the marriage to my father that helped the family a bit. My mum's lobola (dowry) was twenty-one cows and many other items. Now for an ordinary Mosotho, especially in those days (late 60's early 70's), that was big time possession of goods. My father's dad was a rich farmer as I mentioned, owning every domestic animal you can name, every fertile land with massive fields for planting crops, etc. We used to drink milk straight from the cows, even goats—talk about pasteurization. I think the milk used to be boiled only. Every time I visited the village, my grandfather would throw a big mokete (party) in celebration of my coming home. We ate so much meat it was not funny. The good thing is he was quite generous, as he would invite everybody for the meal. People liked meat but could not afford it.

When I see my mum, I see a woman of power and strength, someone who works extremely hard to achieve set goals. So I could not comprehend the kind of childhood she had. I guess that's what gave her the determination—her children would not go through that. To date, my mother is still a hard worker, despite my advising her to slow down a bit. She has not only supported my education, but through education has improved the lives of my uncles, cousins, and other people. My mum is a people's builder in so many ways. I regard her as the best psychologist I have ever known and a very practical, realistic person about life in general. I love her Christian approach to life, one removed from stereotypes of judging, malicious talks, or holier-than-thou attitudes.

When I was a teenager, as all parents panic about the behaviour and attitudes of teenagers, I overheard her conversations with friends and family that the most important tool you can give a child is information in all areas of their life. It was common in those days for parents to check their daughters when they came home from boarding schools as to whether or not they were still virgins (boys have never been tied down on these matters and aren't even today). I do not know how they checked them. All I remember is that my mum used to talk to me about sexuality and the implications of sex, which were disease and unwanted pregnancy. It was a taboo to talk about such things to your children and still is for most of us today. So I do not know how my mum overcame this. She just made me see the importance of education and how all these things would prevent me from such goals. Her famous words used to be "you teach a child principles. They make their own decisions based on sound knowledge." She equally taught me that it was healthy to be friends with both girls and boys. When I think of it, I have had such wonderful friendships with both sexes all my life. I always knew who I was and where I was going, thus I was not bordered by maleness or femaleness of relationships. Of course, I have had my childhood upheavals like any other child. I am not trying to portray perfection here. In fact, that's the one thing I was not and am still not. And do not get a wrong picture; my mum was high on discipline. So I would never get away with mischief without a punishment.

With this healthy approach to relationships between humans, it is not surprising that the boy next door was my best friend. We played together most of the time. One Christmas, I got excited about one thing or another and ran across to his house, unfortunately forgetting the slim, iron fence. It cut me on my left leg (a mark still stands today). It was so funny as we began to tend to what was then an injury. He was like the brother I never had and very good friend. We were sensible, bright, and knew we wanted a good future. So we encouraged each other in general matters of life and on academic grounds. After the "0" levels, he went to the National University of Lesotho to study for a bachelor's degree in arts, while I went to college to study nursing. It was in my mother's handbook that I would become a nurse and then a doctor once I had gained some life skills. I must admit, a career in nursing provides a package in personal as well as professional skills. I loved the sciences especially chemistry and biology, so I was excited that I was going to study about the body's structure and function and the chemistry of life. Some people may say, if this is so true, why did you not stay on and practice nursing or go into medicine? Life is not static; you have to challenge yourself above limits. When I finished my studies as a nurse and a midwife, which took four years, I had no specific area of interest in which to specialize. I still clearly loved being in the health field and had fantasies of being a doctor—a surgeon for that matter. I loved to cut, so surgery would have been my thing. As you will learn in the story, I became an educator in human physiology instead. I enjoyed the physiology lab during my university period and noticed I still particularly liked to cut, even dissecting frogs. When I studied midwifery, I got such satisfaction upon repairing by suturing any tears (episiotomies). I got a joy when the work was done neatly and recovery was speedy. I love what I do today and that my students benefit from the fact that I teach biology with a sound knowledge and understanding of how this subject relates to clinical practice. In fact, my interview presentation was based on demonstrating how biology underpins practice.

Today, people talk about how lonely life must be for "an only child" living thousands of miles from home. The distance from the UK to Lesotho is about 9930.68 kilometres or 6170.64 miles. To be honest, I do not remember growing up feeling as if I missed something. I was always surrounded by people, both family and friends. Everyone was always protecting me with love from one angle or another, or maybe that is what I wanted to see and believe. I never faced any form of social isolation in any place where I had been and lived until I came to Britain. This in no way means that everyone who smiles at you or talks to you has your best interest at heart, even your relatives or best friends, the ones you are trying to protect. I am not good at using negative energy. As far as I know, I always look at the positive side of everyone even when challenged seriously. It is so amazing how people do these things so easily. Life goes on. Some things you have to overlook or else you will put yourself in unnecessary misery.

Chapter Two
Education

It is unfortunate that in resource-poor countries such as Lesotho (and all of Africa), education is not a free commodity. In my time, our parents or guardians paid for our education from primary through college or university. In college/university, the government grants bursaries and sponsorships, but unfortunately uses corruption to grant this depending on who you know, etc. I understand now in Lesotho primary education is free. That is really a great achievement, and the government should be praised for that. I guess that is the reason for such a wide gap between the rich and the poor. On the other hand, the message that seems to be preached in Africa is that the way to success is via book education. A lot of talents go unnoticed and unrefined as no one sees differently and is more complicated by the lack of resources or unwise use of what is available. When you look around the world today, there are a lot of successful people who have not gone through formal education but were channelled in the right direction. Do not get me wrong, education is beautiful, empowering, and literally your mother and father. With it you can reach the sky, explore the world, and simply broaden your horizons.

With her sense of strong determination, my mum did all she could to ensure I would go through all the formal education stages, from preschool, primary, secondary, and high school to collage or university. She knew that this would be my gateway to life—but look I am still not rich. She did not guarantee me this, but a good life. Fortunately, I took her advice and strength seriously. I believed in her and thus was tuned into education. I do not recall all of it, but I remember that when I was about four years old, I lived with her friend who is still a teacher , to go to preschool at a Catholic school. Although my mum did not finish all of her education due to her marriage to my father, she was the best teacher even to date. She went through my work with me in my foundation and secondary years. She has brilliant maths skills, and I have seen her teach all the children in our extended family. I have seen her teach my own children in England, and I think what an amazing woman!

Up until I was in standard five (ten years old), I did not live with my mother during the school days. She was always on the lookout for good schools. So after her friend, I lived with my aunt, who lived closer to a very good Catholic school. I stayed with her for three years, after which I began to complain that I wanted to live with her full-time, not only during holidays. So at the end of that year I moved to the town where she worked and lived. I was enrolled at another good Catholic school. Those years' prior to high school and boarding school were blissful. I have always had good relations with the teachers wherever I have been. I do not know if it was due to my personality and the fact that I rated among the bright ones. Thinking about it now, teachers do tend to like children who are in the forefront at the expense of the others. I now look at my children and realize that unlike me, my daughter is very quiet like my mum, and though bright, she might be forgotten. My son on the other hand is an extrovert like my dad, and I do not have to worry about him. So it made a difference being at school and being liked (I am sure not by everybody). I did not worry about who liked me or did not. I was content with myself and filled with energy to pump into my books. This is the strength I try to teach my children all the time—to love themselves and be content with who they are while they strive to do their very best in their work. In life, you concentrate your energy in the positive direction. My performance at school was always good, above average, so I was happy and saw success coming my way. Honestly, I was not a perfect child, but I was never found among troublemakers. I even used to wonder when and how those who were found in mischief got to do whatever they did.

I do recall once when in high school, a few of us got into some trouble. It was an evening just like any other. We were leaving the study rooms, heading to our boarding house. This was a convent school where the nuns were very strict about everything. The way to the dormitory was through the residence for the nuns. In the middle, there was a punching box that the soldiers used for their exercises. They lived within the institution near our dormitory as the guards for the convent, I guess. We were always to walk very quietly when passing this place. But this particular evening around 21:00, one girl or group of girls lost it, they began to punch this bag, making loud noises, and everybody joined. I had done it too, and was just unlucky and got caught. When the nuns were awakened by the noise, they came out, and I was in the group that was the last to join the feast. So we were called to the matron's house for reprimanding. You see we had denied doing it at first. They asked us to lay down with our bums exposed so we could get a hiding. After a few strokes and some pain, we admitted it. We were given a grilling and went back to sleep. I was so upset with myself, but I guess I was just a normal teenager. My children ask me today if I was ever naughty. I tell them some things but not this one as yet.

Even though the nuns were very strict in every way, it never really bothered me. I was sensible most times, and so was never really in their faces for negative things. I felt the disappointment from them for being foolish at any time, as I was a role model. Thinking about it, it was quite a funny environment, where we were watched over in every aspect, at the dining hall, study rooms, play grounds, you name it. At the time, I was never bothered by or questioned the rules. I was there to learn and that was it. We were in class with boys but separated during play time. It did not make any sense really, as I knew a number of girls who still managed to get together with boys and got pregnant. I am quite a free-living being, and even though law abiding, in some things I like freedom. So, I saw no harm in going to the teachers' houses. But the nuns did not like this, especially with male teachers. There should be standards set to protect the children, I believe. But a certain level of responsibility and trust in children is equally important. I am easy to get along with, so an invitation to a teacher's house was not a surprise. I often went with another pupil. I am not aware if there was a written rule for pupils not to go visiting teachers. You must appreciate that we were controlled in every way possible. Thinking about it now, I see why some kids took to extremes once they had finished there, like payback time. I met one girl who had been at the boarding school during my time in town very drunk to her last breath. When I asked how she got herself to this level, she told me she was angry for the controlling nature of the nuns. That she was now living her life as she pleased. The only thing she did not take into consideration was the fact that it was her life she was ruining. I do realize it was not a very conducive environment for children who probably had other issues. I was not bothered at all at the time.

One summer holiday, we went to get some of my stuff from school with a friend. My math teacher, seeing us pass by, called us in for a little chat. The sisters must have been looking at us from the window. We heard her call out my name to leave the house, which we ignored. She came puffing with such a rage, telling us to leave at once via the convent. This is the one time I recall telling her that her behaviour was uncalled for, that we had a right to talk to people at any place and time. We explained that it was a holiday and we were not under the school management. I had written my final year exams and felt I ought to say something at last. She was not pleased, but at least I had said my piece, too. I wonder if they still do this today.

My mother had already instilled in me the career inclination I would follow when the time came. She always spoke about how I would be a nurse and finally become a doctor. I think for my mum to be a good doctor you had to be a nurse first. Whether at that time she was aware of these disciplines being independent of each, I am not sure. But indeed today it's proven that doctors who have been qualified as nurses are the best doctors. They are more in tune with the holistic care of the patient. A lot of my friends who trained as nurses and went into medicine are fantastic doctors. They seem better at communicating and the general approach to patients and clients, more understanding of psychosocial elements of ill health. So they treat patients more with compassion and understanding of their individual circumstances.

As my mother's dream came true, I followed a career in nursing and midwifery. At that time you had to be a general nurse as well as a midwife to be able to practice. It makes sense due to the nature of the health system, which is carried by nurses with clinician's skills. Nurses are highly qualified in Lesotho and South Africa as they simply run the health services. After a year of working in a neonatal intensive care in a big SA city hospital, I knew that I did not really belong in bedside nursing. Do not get me wrong, I loved it and was fulfilled when the children recovered after days, weeks, and sometimes months of ventilation. But not all of them survived the ordeal depending on lung function and general organ stability. I could not sustain this, even though it was extremely challenging with a very good team of intelligent nurses and doctors. I then began to wonder where I really wanted to be in the field of health.

One thing's for sure, I used to be fascinated by my tutors at the college and used to think reaching their level would be an ultimate for me. It looked so far from reach while I was a student, but now I could see myself touch it. From my school age I was fascinated by human biology, how the body works, and the chemistry behind it. The thought of being a lecturer or educator was not far off. I began to apply to university to enable myself to get into education. When you look for something you will find it. I was accepted into university for a bachelor's degree. Studying human physiology among other things was the highlight for my future career. I knew then that I would teach human physiology in colleges and universities. Amazingly, in my last year of study, the Department of Nursing where I earned my qualification as a nurse contacted me, and offered me a post to teach human physiology. This was the greatest blessing! When I later made the decision to go back to university after a year of working, I did not have money to pay for my studies and the Lesotho government would not pay as I had already been out of the country. My poor mum once again had to support my upkeep while at university. It did not occur to me that she really needed financial support. I was not rich, but I always had what I needed like any other child. So I did not realize my mother could do with my financial help. She always had big dreams to build a bright future for us. At this point she had been ill for many years and was unable to sustain the small business that helped her to get me and my cousins through education. So she was now looking up to me. I felt that I was selfish not to have worked a bit more prior going back to university, but it was too late and she would not let me give up my dreams.

Education is very expensive in most African countries from primary right up to college/university. You may get a sponsor into tertiary education. My mum had toiled and done all these for me, she needed a break. But there I was in need so she continued to work hard and even did child-minding to get by. On this note, I appreciate the work ethic of the western countries whereby a job is a job regardless of its nature. In my country, people class jobs and equate them to social status. Well, it does happen in every society to be realistic; but the outlook might be slightly different. Luckily my mum is a very open-minded person and takes pride in whatever she does.

I faced some financial challenges at university, as all my savings were used up in the first couple of months. But God was always watching over me, because I managed to get a bursary and loan towards the fees for tuition and accommodation. Yes, God watches over you and has a plan for your life if you believe it. I have always been a blessed girl wherever I have been, I meet lots of people who are just like me and provide a friendly environment. So I sailed through my studies as planned, graduating with a bachelor's degree as God opened all the gates.

Young, motivated, happy, and a single woman, I had a serious sense of purpose, I was simply enjoying my life and sharing it with those who embraced life. I was so well balanced with no stereotypes of male versus female; it did not scare me to relate to people from all walks of life. Thanks to my mum. My mother says my character is that of my father. He related to everyone across his way regardless of culture, ethnicity, nationality, etc. Unfortunately, it was his nature that let to the loss of his life. The people simply envied him. When losers look at people of value and envy them, they will try to pull them down in so many ways.

A friend once commented that as soon as I hold an A4-size envelope, busy writing and posting, she knows I am making a move to some place. The time to move had ticked. I always knew I wanted to go either to America or England. My mum knew I was an explorer so was not worried about an only child going so far from home. It would be her chance to explore the world. As it is she has come to England many times. I studied in Cape Town which is about 750 miles (1207.008km) from home. So being away from home is not foreign. Besides I was at a boarding school for five years, college, and university!

Chapter Three
The Move to England

One of the Bible quotations I love is in the book of Ecclesiastes. It was written by King Solomon, the son of David, the man in whom all known wisdom sat as a gift from God. He describes that in life there is time for everything: to live, be happy, be upset, to stay, to leave, etc. So yes, for me it was time to explore the Western world. There are many theories that people use to describe migration of African people to the Western world. Some unexposed people make assumptions that it must be due to the poverty crisis in Africa, that we are all running away from this calamity! While there are some realities on the poverty crisis in Africa, like in other third-world, poor countries such as Peru, India, etc., the majority of Africans come here in search of education and professional jobs. Unfortunately, even those with some good educational background, the reality of the job market or how the system classes their achievements, makes them settle for less. Some end up with care work, restaurants, super-markets, and many such clergy jobs (the so-called working class). A good number strives to get into higher education to retrain into other professions.

There is a group that comes to the UK to flee their home circum-stances caused by political issues. On the other hand, my coming to Britain was not related to African crisis like many other people in the same circle. I came to England to pursue my life's dream of exploring other worlds. I have always known that I am an explorer with a drive to experience new things! So I came with an education to explore a new way of life. Of course I was disillusioned like most people, thinking that the power of the sterling pound would give me the ultimate dream life, a big house with massive garden, swimming pool/Jacuzzi, top-of-the-range car, etc. Oh, not so fast. The cost of living is very high as you learn very quickly.

One holiday in December of 1996, I made a trip to England for a visit. It was during this time that I decided I would come back to work and study in England. The pound was so attractive and I thought I would love to touch it in the future. I had done my time of service in the Department of Nursing, so when I gave notice of my intentions to go abroad, there was no hesitation. They would still have loved me to stay, but my time was up since I felt a need for something different.

In preparations to move to England, I had made inquiries as to the easy way to get a job. At that time the agencies recruiting nurses to the UK were many. I had already planned that before I could work at a college or university as a lecturer, I would love to understand the health system first. I then registered with an agent that would get me a job in a hospital or community. Little did I realize the implications of this—I could be sent to different places at any time, whether a clinic, hospital, or specialised unit like intensive care, in accordance with my skill set. I had registered with the United Kingdom Central Council (UKCC), which is now the Nursing and Midwifery Council (NMC). The tickets were bought, farewell to friends and family underway, and off I flew to the UK My family and friends saw me off at Maseru-Moshoeshoe 1 International Airport. Nobody, including my mother, was alarmed by my move as they had seen it coming for a long time. I have always stayed away from home as mentioned. My mother set me up for independence early to prepare me to deal with the world as an only child. She always worried about me being able to strive for myself in case anything happened to her. She did have ill health during my high school years—thank God she lives on today above the age of sixty. At the airport, there were no tears as I had warned everyone I wouldn't want anyone crying. My connecting flight to London's Heathrow Airport would be in Johannesburg, and off I went.

Arriving at Heathrow on that chilly morning in February of 2000, I knew then that I was beginning another chapter of my life very far away from home. This is what I had asked for, so there was no going back. I was not depressed or sad but there was a deep sense of loneliness and of being alone. Those feelings were a challenge that I had to overcome. Someone from the agency was waiting for me at the airport, so that was quite nice. It was a shock looking at all those old buildings with no sense of attraction whatsoever. Now I know it is the character inherent in their designs that defines them. No wonder the expression says "do not judge the book by its cover." The illusion becomes a reality. Most people from Africa and other third-world countries think of England and America as having streets of gold and immaculate top-of-the range buildings. No! Reality hits you.

The agent drove me to what was going to be my temporary accommodation. My God, I nearly had a heart attack! It was a little room within a family's house. I wondered how on earth anybody could be expected to live in such a room. I was used to space and class. It then began to dawn on me that a friend I had met from home who came from England had been going on about how cosy, classy, and simply beautiful my place was. He went on to explain that I would pay a fortune to live in such a luxurious house in England. It is true that people back home only think of "state of the art" living in the Western countries, especially the UK and USA I could not last in that place for a couple of days, so I asked to be rehoused. To be fair, the family was very nice and offered to include me in family meals at the cost of twenty pounds, excluding the rent, which was seventy pounds per week. It was a strange arrangement I must admit. In our culture, there is just not a way where a stranger can live in a household with its members on a daily basis. The second arrangement was better but not the kind of place I would want to settle for. Going around these places and people's houses, I realized that this is a typical British way of life for the majority, even the very elite with good jobs. Off course, just like in any society, there are people who live in big houses with a massive amount of land (the other class). I began to realize that accommodations in England were some of the most expensive basic needs. Most people, even professionals, share accommodation to reduce the cost. The reality, therefore, is the pound is not worth much in England. It is only outside of the UK that its value is appreciated. I finally moved to Middlesex and found a room in a beautiful family home with an en suite bathroom, which suited me fine. I lived with the female owner, and we soon became good friends. We used to chat about life in general. She was a lecturer in linguistics, and so was highly exposed to culture, ethnicity, and the rest. We are still in touch to date. It is through her that I learned a little bit about the culture of the English people, which she despised funny enough. Later on as I mixed and worked with the English people, I understood why she despised the culture. I learned how personal space was extremely important, even verging on loneliness. We had misunderstandings, but the good thing is that we always resolved the issues in one way or the other. At this time, this was normal, and there were no racial issues. I had not been sensitized on this yet. She would talk about the English people and their miserable selves, how they have shaped other people's way of life through colonization. Reflecting on this, yes, as a child I was impacted by the English ways. To be successful at school, you had to speak and write English very well. You were considered high class if you were well spoken in English. It is still a norm up to today to some extent in Africa and other non-English-speaking countries.

The discussions we had about different people were never centered on colour or ethnicity. She was a well-exposed lady who had mingled with other nationalities. So racial issues were never part of our discussion or concern. So when did I begin to see prejudice in people based on colour? Before I got a job in one of the universities as a senior lecturer, I had worked in various clinical settings with people from different ethnic backgrounds. I began to see an unwritten discrimination/prejudice based on colour. The problem is that you cannot prove this even if you were to take it any further. I generally get along with other people as I relate well and know my grounds. So no one can really pin me down due to error of intelligence. But I know a couple of times when a colleague would undermine my knowledge till otherwise proved by evidence when challenged. It was so baffling for me that people were so engraved with prejudice. This is what all people in my box have to do: prove themselves before the natural acknowledgement of just being a human being. Barak Obama, in his book *Dreams From My Father,* described how being black was a challenge in itself. You face so much negative pressure, it can only make you strong—what cannot break you will make you strong. Many great, black, successful people like Oprah, Martin Luther King, etc. have gone through the same cruel measures. You would have hoped that we would now be on a different page. But no, it is a continuing reality. It's like teaching people about healthy lifestyles to avoid illness, yet the pattern continues. You cannot stop educating people regardless—so we have to continue educating people on equality and diversity.

After about a year in a hematology unit, I knew it was time to move onto full-time education. My love of biology was always prominent as I had a keen interest in teaching students and building on their biological knowledge to apply to practice. I began to look for lecturer positions in human physiology. I wrote to a number of universities where such adverts were posted. The first university that I went to for an interview was in an absolutely perfect location. I would be near the sea. The job offer was challenging, and I was extremely excited even when I went to the interview. I could smell and picture myself among the academics there making a difference. I was quite confident through the interview process, and truly I cannot recall the reason they did not offer me the post, something pertaining to a lack of experience teaching in a UK university. I did not get discouraged despite people discouraging me, saying there are higher chances of me winning the lottery than being given such a post—based on colour discrimination. For me such concepts sounded farfetched as I was removed from colour orientation or consciousness. I wanted to prove that I would get any job that I wanted as long as I had the qualifications for it. I was one hundred percent geared to find the job I had been trained to do and do it really well. Before I was appointed as a senior lecturer in biological studies at a particular university, I had two or three more interviews from other universities in England. To those that short-listed me for the interview, even though some turned me down, it was such an experience. I am not someone who gives in to failure or get easily discouraged by circumstances. It is in fact such situations that give me a serious drive to get what I want and believe I deserve. Of course, in one form or another, I had a tendency to think that my skin colour may have had an impact on getting my post, as by now people had rubbed it into me so much. I had to fight such feelings away and focus. At this stage, I had seen some prejudice as mentioned earlier.

The obsession did stay on my mind in one way or another. On the day of the interview for the university that offered me the post, I arrived there early via the reception. I wanted to find out how many candidates were short-listed for the post (senior lecturer in biological studies). There were more than a handful of candidates for one post. I recall thinking, "I am the only one with a non-English surname. Will this be applicable?"

As people, we all go through lots of experiences where you wonder whether colour or ethnicity really played a part. In a way, my way of thinking was slowly changing from hearing all these incidences. Well, I must have impressed the panel as I was offered the post. I was absolutely ecstatic! An opportunity had presented itself, and I was determined to do my very best. A dream had come true. The same myth that everything good comes from the West made me overly excited— a senior lecturer at a UK university. Nothing could beat this thought at the time. I saw an opportunity to improve my academic as well as personal development. It was a call for me to read wider, deeper, and share with the students this profound knowledge. These ideas were crushed not long after being in the job. The education system was very different to where I came from. The students were not keen on acquiring an in-depth knowledge with a few exceptions. They complained about the high level of biology I was teaching. I used to get emails claiming I was not considerate to the less intelligent students. I had rough months in the beginning, facing even perditions about how my accent made it difficult for students to understand the subject. This was one of the things that made me label things in colour—how weird! My future of challenge with demand on research was almost crumbling, but it picked up later. I kept my spirit up with encouragement from the dean. She liked my ambition and identified with the force of experience I had and the passion to share it. She kept my spirit up with encouragement both on a professional and personal level whenever we met. To date, she remains a special person in my life.

In general, the students were not so education hungry like the ones I had taught back home. You see, for them, they understood that education was the only escape to better life. In a resource-rich country, the mentality is different, no one goes hungry because they are not educated, and the national service will cater for basic needs. Rather, they complain about everything. I learned that the approach to education was completely different. I began to wonder whether in poor countries like mine, the education system was designed to make it hard for people to achieve in life. The same systems that had been adopted via colonization seemed to be harder and unfair to these underprivileged countries. I never worried about this since I love education, the harder the better (hard to believe)! Was I learning something to take back and apply?

To get into an institution of higher learning back in Africa is very tough. The selection criteria is a very high academic requirement. For instance, entry into university for nursing requires four credits (including English, science, and maths) and any two passes. English, unfortunately, is still a gateway to education as a result of colonization. No wonder education is still viewed through the eyes of the Western ideology.

To my surprise, the same standards do not apply in the UK, and yet there is a general classification of the African system as being lower than the UK. This is where we can truly see the power of money and economic stability. The education system in Africa is made hard to impossible, and yet no resources exist to support those who may not have an academic mind, who are equally talented in different aspects. This leads to loss of potential skills which could be developed for a better Africa.

Chapter Four
Culture Shock

As mentioned earlier, my ambition began to decline after a couple of months in my new job due to the nature of the education system, the attitudes, and prejudice, etc. It did not take me long to notice that everyone was called by their first name whether you were the dean, head of department, senior, or junior lecturer. This familiarity gave the professional relationships almost no barriers at all in my opinion. I found it difficult, because it seemed a student could say anything they pleased to a lecturer. I faced so much stress it was amazing. The students challenged my knowledge with sarcasm like "you are so knowledgeable. Did you obtain your degree in England?" The implication was nothing great can come out of Africa. If you have some knowledge then the English will have taught you. Well, lack of exposure and knowledge is a big factor in people's attitudes towards others. You just have to blame it to their ignorance and feel sorry for them. I got petitioned once about the complexity and abstract nature of how I taught biology. In a meeting to deal with such complaints with senior staff members, it was clear the support was given to the students as one member commented how if she/he was a first year student nurse and was given such high level of biology she/he would have freaked out! I was even more amazed at the lack of support for a new member of staff from management, how my ambition was being crushed. I was cruelly told how the students were not taking a first degree in biology or medicine, that they needed basic biology to underpin practice. I knew this concept long before; I had taught similar students the same subject for couple of years. I am teachable, so I knew I had to reconstruct my manner of teaching. I guess it is good to be adaptable. This was a reality shock, but I knew quitting was not an option. I have the philosophy that quitting is for cowards and that I would never leave any job because of another person. Well, I guess it depends on the nature of the problem. I know there are times where perhaps quitting because of another person may be the only option as continuing might just be self-damaging. People cope differently in a given situation—so I would not judge a person for making such a decision.

I began to question myself in relation to racial issues, wondering whether I was being judged on those terms. I was not all that naive. I had listened, observed, and probably even seen how these things can impact people. It is simply that I refused to succumb to such.

With time, I learned that it was not so much the level of biology but rather the perception of what they thought they needed to be learning. I investigated the nature of how biology was taught in the past and whether there were similar complaints. Luckily, someone had done a pilot study that addressed similar problems. It was clear that most of the students found biology their biggest challenge. I also realized that in England a science/maths was not necessarily a prerequisite to getting into the course. So you had students with varied biology backgrounds or none. A light shone on me, therefore, that more challenges were still to come. Some were genuine, others purely provocative. You had to be so extremely careful in maintaining professionalism when dealing with such sarcasm. One student asked whether I would lose my job if she/he failed biology. Honestly, how does anybody ask such questions? Luckily all the challenges about my knowledge of the subject matter would not scare me at all—that was the one thing I was on top of. I am not implying that I know everything. Any intelligent person knows that. But it was quite an experience.

God gave me the strength I needed to deal with it. Far away in a foreign world, the last person I would tell was my mother. She would worry herself to high blood pressure. Talking to friends helped me through the ordeal. The one thing I was not going to lose was my self-esteem, dignity, or self-respect in any way. I became even stronger while I understood the bitterness of blacks/minorities fighting against a regime that put us in an inferiority box, a regime that says skin colour speaks louder than words, where you have to fight to be heard and recognized. This was not the kind of a world I wanted, but it was a reality. I look beyond these things, as they do not describe my world. When I felt the need, I faced management and prayed for sanity at all levels of challenging situations.

The saddle of discrimination is felt by everybody in my box. Being undermined, being disregarded by both those holding higher and lower positions around you is the daily routine. The number of times some of the staff members still thought I was one of the students or called me by the name of the other black member of staff, demonstrated that to them you are just a black person probably with no name or one they could not be bothered to learn. After five years of going to the university library, staff that I had met many times still believed

I was one of the students. I stopped explaining as there was no point. It was clear they were not interested.

I recall from many of the incidences how one of the service men from the campus literally came to me with a disgusting attitude about where my car was packed. I was wrong, but it was no manner to talk to another human being. He just felt he could undermine me anyhow he pleased, calling me "woman." He said he thought I was a student. Even if I was, where was the human respect? All he saw was a black woman on whom he could exercise his powers. When I took it up, it was my word against his, and some report from his boss said that he was not that kind of a person. It was a pointless battle, and he died before the end of the disputes, which was such a shame really. No, I was not rejoicing over it. But you can appreciate how awful this whole thing seemed. Prejudice goes such a long way in our society. The list can go on and on. Once in one of the biology labs, I accidentally broke one of the pieces of equipment. The service guy had a nasty attitude, telling me how I need to repay the damage—oh Lord of mercy, what is wrong with people? I am not silly; I knew he would have been gentle had it been another white staff member. Of course I stood my ground with him and earned his respect after a while. It is almost like they want to see how human you are to earn the same respect they require from you. After a long time of battle, you begin to relate well to some extent but are constantly reminded you do not belong. And of course, by this time you know only too well you have to watch your back. The smile, or the teeth rather, means nothing really!

Lots of people experience similar abuse based on prejudice. If only we could all write our stories the list would be so long! I would love one day to compile stories of various people's experiences as evidence that cannot be denied. A friend faced a situation of dispute between herself and her manager where confrontation had started rudely from the manager. During the initial meeting with human resources, which I was allowed to attend for support as my friend's English was not well developed, the whole meeting was so biased, so manipulative, it was ridiculous. Out of the blue, the manager claimed she had witnesses who had seen how she screamed at her without respect. As I had to write a statement on behalf of my friend, I questioned some of the inconsistencies portrayed, but I did not get any tangible answer to substantiate the allegations. The irony of it was that she told me they were the only two people in the office when the manager shouted at her. So where did the manager get a witness who even agreed to this? An inquiry was to be set up, but at this point, my friend wanted to leave her job as she felt extremely mistreated and worried that the staff would team up with the manager to give her complete hell. I encouraged her to go to a lawyer with her case, as it was a chance for her to get a fair sentence. All she said was, "You know these people will just smile while they all crucify me." I understood her, but I knew it was not time to give up. People are different as I mentioned, so for her quitting was the only option, sad as it was. For some, a negative environment makes them quit, while for some it becomes a motive to strive for balance in this unfair society. That is the one job I would definitely not give up on.

I felt the pain that we can only understand when people literally twist information at the expense of another. It reminded me an experience at the school, where a woman reversed into my car, leaving a dent. She was so shocked, and she had lots of kids to drop at school. When I asked that we call the police, she said she would give me her insurance details. So we exchanged numbers. To my shock, that evening when we had agreed to resolve the matter, I was called by her husband, who then told me a long story of how his wife did not hit me. It was pointless arguing with a fool, so I let it pass. You may say road rivalry is common between people regardless of who is involved. But in the way the husband spoke to me, though he was not even on the scene, you smelled arrogance of a different nature.

We describe culture as customs a certain society abides by to understand norms in their immediate environments. I wonder sometimes whether it is the culture of white people to ignore those that they do not belong with, specifically with skin colour, or to treat you differently, just because you are indeed different? Or is mostly an attitude isolated to the English? Some of my white friends and acquaintances who are not from England also talk of some similar experiences of not being accepted by their English white peers. They are the ones who came up with the notion that "variety is the spice of life," but clearly they do not really like variety, at least not in the true sense of the word. It is in this same society that the issue of promoting culture and diversity is a benchmark. It is one thing to talk about something, and it is yet another to practice it.

Let's face it, work is work, and negativism in how management treats people may be similar across or beyond racial orientation. You see your colleagues who are white suffer similar stresses or abuse. But some experiences make you interpret things in the light of colour discrimination on a comparative scale. Being committed to your work is highly important to the smooth running of any institution. But when there are personal, pressing issues, whether ill health, social problems, etc., good managers will look at this without putting a face to the job and objectively assess why an individual may not have accomplished a task in time. There was one situation where there was an issue that let to my inability to complete a task, and I was attacked as a person instead of addressing what was at hand. It is unfortunate that the manager at the time had discussed me maliciously with another staff member, not realizing that I was close by and heard every word. The words were obviously of a person expressing that they did not care how ill I was or about whatever was going on, all they needed was for me to accomplish the task at any expense. I had already made attempts regarding how I would go about it with the immediate line manager. A big lesson was learned here as I made a complaint to the highest level. As the truth was obvious, before we had a chance to discuss this issue, the manager had resigned. I was not rejoicing over that as all I wanted was both parties to iron things out and learn a new way to move forward. I got on with life, as it is my philosophy to look ahead not behind a closed door. I also learned that I should record everything that took place around my work, whether big or small. I realized that I was now making a move away from the humane approach, but becoming legally wise as I had to watch my steps all the time. It was too clear to me that colour talks louder than words—whether people deny it or not. I was not filling up with hatred, rather amazement at the reality show I was in. You embrace those who embrace you no matter how superficial they are and move on.

In general, people in the UK keep to themselves as a way of life. When you are travelling by train into London for instance, everyone is reading a paper, book, or magazine or engaged in some form of electronic device to avoid any small talk with others whether black or white. They love their space, and that is their culture. In my country, people talk to each other instead. In Noel Edmonds's *Positively Happy: Cosmic Ways to Change Your Life, he* cites from an article in *The Guardian*, stating that "half the UK population avoids making small talk with strangers." These strangers are not just shadowy figures on the street, but actually their own neighbours, customers in local shops, fellow parents at school gates, and colleagues at work. Even as I write this book, I do not know the names of my neighbours on either side of my house. We simply wave at each other over the fence or if I happen to be on the driveway when they are outside. Engaging with other people opens doors for self-discovery and enriches your character. So for those people who shut themselves away from others because they are too stuck up on colour, really miss out the fullness of life and its spices.

A friend said to me once that one of the reasons why British people ignore you even at the school gates is that they are afraid of the unknown. This fear of the unknown for me is colour coded, because with time, they seem to merge well with other white people from outside of Britain while you still stand as an outsider. I have never lived in a country that had such a severe sense of isolation. You experience this at work, social gatherings, at school drop offs, etc. Everyone seems to keep to themselves or belongs to some clique group. Today this person greets you, tomorrow they pretend they have not met you. This beats me. I do not struggle to have social relations, but I cannot stand people who seem to ignore you with intention. And I definitely will not push myself where I am clearly not wanted, neither will I fall prey to someone by seeking some acceptance. I accept who I am, and that is enough. You cannot be a friend to everyone obviously, but being civil is cool. Well, somebody better tell me if I have made a wrong assumption. No matter how sociable or likable you are, in one way or another you start to feel the air of discrimination. You only escape this when it is in one-to-one conversation. When it's a crowd of more than two, you become less significant unless you have had a long, established relationship of some sort with these people, even in its nature of superficial fulfilment. I do understand to some extent that in our isolation, some of the black folk try hard to hold onto someone who may make them feel they fit in the circle while trying hard to earn their approval.

Don't call me a racially oriented person, as I am not. Once some black folks or so-called people of colour believe they have gained friendship with the white folk, they will go out of their way to lick behind them and treat you cold in their midst. You are only good friends away from that. Now what do you call that? It is a result of the slave mentality as an unknown author puts it. I just cannot understand this way of thinking. While I am not suggesting there is anything wrong with people relating across cultural, biological, or racial boundaries, I get concerned when people fail to embrace their own. It makes me wonder whether they love themselves enough to belong there. It reminds me of Barak Obama, facing similar challenges as a young boy. He shares an experience where in a white-dominated school in his class, there was another black child, but they both simply ignored each other as they "watched from a distance." He says that it was "as if direct contact would only remind us more keenly of our isolation." (*Dreams From My Father*, 2004).

Indeed, black people continue to ignore each other as they strive for acceptance, especially in a society of whites. Black people are generally outspoken. That is who we are, and there is definitely nothing wrong with it as long as it causes no disruptions. During the school sports days, I am among those who cheer loudly, and sometimes people will come up to me, acknowledging that it's good to hear people keeping the grounds alive. In conforming to the white standards, I recall how one woman on the school grounds indicated to me how I should not speak loudly when I came to her with some excitement. I was not even overly loud—just being me. She was clearly feeling embarrassed that we were in the midst of white people so I had to pretend to be something else to belong. I was quite disgusted and did feel sorry for her instead. In a lot of ways it has to do with self-esteem and how the view of oneself among other people.

A friend, who is very analytical about behaviour, once mentioned to me that the one thing that the white people have over the black folk is disruption of unity. Think about the era of slavery, how black man sold another black man in exchange for some useless goods. In unity, there is power! If you break that, the systems will falter. Unfortunately, even today we are still being controlled by this mentality whether we admit it or not. I do notice at times even among my friends, students, and acquaintances, that some of us are still trying so hard to belong to people who clearly do not think much of us. One black girl in particular, bless her, she had tried so hard to belong with her white friends— she probably grew up in the UK, and that's the only society she was exposed to, but she clearly did not belong. Even the most unintelligent person will make the observation that when it comes to white minority among black, they do not feel it, because in general, black people are accommodating of them, almost like our masters in slavery—how foolish! It is true that in most marriages between black and white people, the relationship works better when the white person yields to the black people than the other way around. I said if I married a white man, he would have to be black for it to work, because I would not attempt to be white.

Despite all obvious racial prejudice, in the majority of cases it has nothing to do with hatred towards a particular person. It is a lack of education. It is more of a collective classification of those who do not belong to a certain group. Without any reasonable doubt, if anything happened to me such as sickness, my colleagues will go out of their way to ensure I get appropriate help. The same people who, in other situations, forget I exist. If anyone asked my colleagues about what kind of a person I am, they will say a lot of positive things about me. That is why I find it weird to understand how prejudice operates. It is almost written on people's hearts to portray attitudes of dislike or non-acknowledgement of outsiders. People do it even without thinking.

Chapter Five
Cost of Living

Unlike the myth that once you are in England you will prosper into a better life, the reality is the shock of how much it costs you to live in this resource-rich country. I guess we have to keep the pound circulating within the country. I have given you a rough idea of how much it cost me to live in a box room for those days I stayed with a family. Do not get me wrong. There are people who live large, luxuriously, like you will find in any country. But generally, the most expensive commodity in UK is accommodation. It made me understand why most people will rent a room out of their family home to cover some other costs. People at home in Africa, on the other hand, believe you are making fortunes, and thus you can share some of your money. A pound is clearly worth nothing when you live in the UK—but if you make it to the top, then you are in the best position in the world. The truth is that opportunities are laid out for everybody who wants to make use of them. I may be judgmental on this note, but I am still puzzled by the fact that in a country where education is free, at least up to high school, there is still so much illiteracy in this country, far away from the myth that everyone who can speak English is classed as elite. Unfortunately in my country, due lack of exposure and the colonization effects, people equate speaking English to education. Of course, you can always tell the difference in the spoken word how the two classes speak. However some people, even though having not gone to school, are very rich. I have come across the rich who tell me plainly they have never had a formal education or dropped out of school at a certain age.

One of the challenges of living in England is child-care expenses for those under five. You literally work so you can pay somebody to look after your children. At the time when I was enquiring about the high number of women who do not work, I discovered that some women choose to be stay-home mums to look after their kids instead of working to pay someone. Of course some have the money, so they do not need to work for an income to earn a living. My kids are now eleven and nine, and at the time when they needed nursery, we paid about £650-700 per child per month. I must admit, my mum helped a great deal on this. She even took them to live with her in Lesotho for a year. The trouble is that within that year I made about four trips to see them. It makes sense therefore that majority of women choose to be stay home mums. It depends pretty much on individual circumstances of literacy or illiteracy as well as financial security.

At the school-going age of five, education is free in state schools. Depending on the county (indicating the local council or municipality) you are in, you may be lucky and get your children in really good state schools, and they would still have the academic capacity to get into grammar school system (GSS). The GSS schools are designed for the academic "creams" of the crop. It does not however mean that those kids who do not pass their *Eleven Plus* exam are any less intelligent. Unfortunately, Examinations, even though they remain the popularly used form of assessment, are not always fair. Highly capable children still fail to make it in these examinations. But yes, I agree with using them. The majority of parents will even relocate to get near good schools, the schools with not only an academic reputation of good results, but also general management of the school in behaviour. Other parents still choose private education for their children. When we viewed private schools when the kids were three and five years old, I fell in love with the school my kids still attend today though my son had to go to another school at the age of seven. The general dynamics of how education is delivered, their mission, and their motto, "Happy, Confident, and Successful Learner," were quite attractive. I knew instantly that that would be my school of choice, the only down side being boys leave at age seven. It was a big sacrifice, as we did not have the kind of money the majority of parents who opt for private education have, but it is a decision I will never regret. Of course some parents make some sacrifices driven by a belief they are getting the best education.

To be honest, I never thought there were underprivileged people in this part of the Globe! You may think, "You are so daft!" I had an understanding that there would be different classes like anywhere, but not at the poor level of conditions people still live in such a resource-rich country. I guess it is a similar myth for the unexposed that "nothing good can come out of Africa." People think we live on trees. It was such a bluff when someone during my first visit to the UK in 1996, asked me whether I bought my clothes in the airport as I arrived in Heathrow. Now that is way beyond ignorance and exposure. I do not know what to call it!

You can appreciate that by the time my kids were ready for school, I was now well aware of the reality of education in England, away from the myth "everything good comes from the English system."

Chapter Six
Survival

A good friend once said, "Motho u fetoloa ke batho": people can change you. Have you ever told yourself that no matter what situations you come across in your life you will never let anyone change you? Oh yes, we all have in one form or another some determination to maintain who we are. The reality is that we are shaped, moulded, by our life experiences, the social networks we belong to, the ordinary man on the street, the powerful leaders, etc. So yes, all these have an impact on you as a person and how you view and deal with life. But for me, the main thing is ensuring I am still myself at the end of the journey, no matter how smooth or rough it may be. A friend who simply followed horoscopes began to believe in everything they predicted. She began to change her life in accordance with these predictions. Unfortunately, she became somebody else that we could not understand. I have always wondered if she understood her life. How could all of that be accurate when the astronomers are querying the accuracy of these stars anyway?

Within ten months in England, I visited home and shared my experience with friends and family. One of my friends was listening attentively with disbelief as I explained how I had developed a mechanism to deal with people at work and social gatherings differently as a survival tool (I guess we all do). But you see, with me, it was a bit more personal as I didn't expect this sort of behaviour or attitude from people based on nothing but colour of the skin. I realized that if you act normal, they will take no notice of you. Always watch your back in case you're misunderstood. It's so hard to pin down some of the incidences to serve as an example to illustrate what I am referring to. The ethic is completely different. I came from a background where I was taught that a dispute has to be resolved between you and the one involved before involving a third party. That was the order of things for me. I never understood the fact that if there is an error or misunderstanding, before you know it, the issue will be with management and everywhere. It seemed always as if people are just waiting to pull you down at all times. More like the so-called "Chinese Whispers." Some people may do it to gain better positions.

A situation once occurred where students had complained about me to another lecturer. The complaint was something along the lines of having made some harassment of a student in my class. Recalling the incident of this nature, I was extremely upset, as the particular student had been rude in my class. Rightfully, I put her to order right there and then, in the presence of others. But she had gone on and lobbied with friends to support that I ridiculed her in class. Personally, as well as professionally, anyone who knows me will know I am not anywhere close to any such kind of behaviour. I would not under any given circumstance be rude or ridicule anyone. Of course I equally would not let anyone walk all over me as I mentioned in the other chapters. To my amazement, I was called in by the manager about this as the colleague whom the student concerned went to report to had gone straight to management. Naturally, I would have expected the lecturer to first come to me to get my side of the story prior going so far. With this, they had concluded that whatever the student said was legitimately correct. I was extremely upset due to the manner of how this issue was dealt with. During this meeting, I made it perfectly clear that I didn't appreciate the whole scenario. I expressed the depth of my disappointment with the management and what was clearly a lack of support.

Clearly our industry is about supporting in the best way the students' learning experience. We put them as our top priority. My philosophy supports the idea of empowering others for success regardless of the colour of their skin. Unless there is some conspiracy, most of my students know that I have their best interests for their learning experience. Generally, people complain about this or the other. So no matter what you do, some students will still complain and find a way to blame lecturers for their failure.

For me this incident had racial discrimination written all over it. I learned later that this same student at the graduations was awarded something for having performed well under strenuous circumstances. Life is like that sometimes, depending on who your connections are even in a society of political correctness. It was such a shock to learn that it implied I made this student's life difficult. There was something about her parents having strong links with the university and sponsoring some of the resources. Who knows the truth? So obviously it was at the best interest of the university to give her maximum cover. I will never really know what went down. Even though I was surprised, I knew I had to keep going, keep moving on my journey of life with a determination to do the right things, but to take no nonsense from anybody.

We all, as elite people, read the same books on management styles, and I have yet to find a writer who agrees with the notion of acting on information provided by only one party. It is true that what is normal for one person may be abnormal for the other person. But I do refer to this behaviour as unprofessional—at least not "Ubuntu," that is lacking the humane element. I gave up trying to fit into a society that treats you as if you do not exist. Do your work, talk to those who acknowledge your presence, and simply live. You have to develop a mechanism to deal with what faces you without being a bitter or bad person. You have to prove yourself worthy all the time; your opinions are disregarded even if they give you a chance for your voice to be heard; and yet the big picture is equality and diversity.

In a meeting that called for ideas, suggestions, and opinions about a certain move and how it would affect staff, I swear to God, my hand was held up so high for a long time, but the chair decided to ignore me. You think I backed down? Oh no! I continued to raise it higher to the point of embarrassment for others in the room. So someone said, "she has had her hand up prior to so many." Finally I was given a chance to voice my ideas. The question became the subject of major consideration, as it transpired, it was a concern for all of us. Why? Naturally, I could have got fed up and left the room, but that is not my style. How long can one really fight for their voice to be heard? It is the same struggle blacks have faced and will continue to face till the end of time. It does make you stronger, but it is not everyone who can face up to this pressure. We talk about affirmative action, equality, and fairness, but it will never happen. It will just be a political correctness written down in black and white but never applied. I do not know if people who are doing this are even aware of it, or if it has become so much a part and parcel of their lives that they will not stop at any time to think about the impact of this on others. I began to understand why some people in my box lost interest to attend some of the meetings. One always jokes that some of these committees, these meetings are for the "important." It is very disheartening indeed. Lucky for me, I always try to look beyond the present and have never felt a need to fight for a position. I am just on a journey leading somewhere.

Experience teaches me that with confrontation, there is never an admittance or ownership of such attitudes. It remains an illusion to think white people will ever treat or regard non-white people as equals, whatever equals mean. I am not striving to be equal with another human being, but I fight for my own rights when it comes to that. We are all human first with same organs. The anatomy is exactly the same. I had never wondered whether as human beings we are the same inside anatomically. Even at university when we studied structure of the human body; we used cadavers that were both black and white. It never shocked me or anything. But I must say I found it so funny when one person who was not in a medical field changed careers and joined the field. During an operation in the theatre, he was shocked that the white person looked exactly like a black person inside. He was genuine, though I could not believe his thinking. People in general do wonder about these things. Innocently, a child who is a friend of my daughter asked me what colour would appear under my skin if I got a cut. This was no doubt emanating from a lack of exposure and simply an inquisitive mind. I fully respect people who deserve my respect despite their skin colour.

When I grew up, there was a notion that "tsoeu ha li tsoane," but "ntso lia tsoana." This means that white people will always stick together when there is an outsider, whereas black people do not stick together. We try everything to avoid each other while we seek acceptance from the white man. I must admit that in my observation living in the UK, Asian people mostly do stick together. When they have a business, they hire their own people at large. No wonder they succeed as a collective. We do have to accept that there is subjectivity in humans that is not always colour coded. They look out for each other. They understand that success is not measured in individual terms.

The discrepancy of how conflicts, misunderstandings, and general issues are dealt with is so obvious even though you are unable to pin anything down as a proof. Many times people will complain about racism at work, social gatherings, church, and institutions. Even though you are sure it exists as you experience it, unless you prove it, it is just another unheard voice. There is a lot of cushioning for a white person compared to a black person on similar accounts. Some people even quit their jobs. Unfortunately, it is very difficult to prove things of this nature unless they are really severe. To be fair, people can experience similar stresses at work regardless of colour. And sometimes it is a quick assumption to make that you are not being treated in a certain manner due to your skin colour. In other words, the minority can abuse the legal knowledge of protection against racial discrimination.

In the era of the slave trade, it was a black man who sold another black man to the whites in exchange of stupid things. There is power in unity, and unity is the only way you can conquer. Look at Africa today, a very rich continent with huge natural resources, but people are dying of hunger and disease as the power struggle continues due to greed, jealousy, and the fight for positions. When will they channel this into positive energy that will benefit the people? The rich and powerful are busy investing in the Western worlds, maintaining white superiority. This will never end. I look at us blacks, how we relate to each other across the globe. There is a notion of comparison: blacks from the Caribbean are under the notion they are superior to black

Africans, and black Africans consider them products of slavery with no education. No unity or embracing of each other as people who share originality. Prejudice is a human element even among any other groups of people, but as a black woman, I wish for unity with my people and not for racial superiority over others. It would make sense that, as a people, we acknowledge one another. Today we talk about black power, black attitude, etc. The reality is had we naturally accepted each other, the leaders would not be fighting so hard for our unity. One friend mentioned in passing about how a specific black Caribbean person had black African hatred. I thought about it and realized that ignorance will continue till eternity if prejudice lingers.

Like many in my bracket, when I was faced with all these challenges, my way of life was to put up a brave front all the time to avoid being the subject of abuse, racially or otherwise. I then noticed in depth that these people have superficial smiles. It is an act or perhaps a norm that has lost its meaning. In essence, they simply show you their teeth when truly they do not see you. I have already stated that maybe it is a cultural thing to close oneself from those you deem as not belonging with you. Being afraid of others has an implication that one is actually afraid of their own self and is deprived of fuller experiences across all nations.

At any place in one's life, nobody wants to be belittled in any form, but I have faced some of these things. Everyone is a specialist in his or her particular subject. IT skills are not my expertise; that's the reason there is support at any work environment. Once, to belittle me I would conclude, a senior colleague asked during a formal meeting with me to demonstrate on her PC where a particular page was located on the university website. Feeling pushed and unable to think clearly, I came closer to the PC and began to flick through. Before much progress, she told me to leave it, as "it was too painful" watching me. You can imagine how I felt: insulted, humiliated, and ridiculed, even though I let it pass. I promised myself that such a thing would never happen to me, but I succumbed to it again. I told one of the union members who suggested I take it up. I decided to leave it this time around. In another incident (I think she was enjoying this), I was asked to locate a particular document. I refused point-blank, saying I would forward the document from my own PC. I explicitly expressed how I felt and that it was a very inappropriate and unprofessional demand from her. And I told her that I thought a manager's role was to support and not give negative criticism, rather positive criticism. I was clearly upset, and she began to apologise. I am sure that had I been in a position to ask them to teach my biology class, it would have been equally unreasonable! When you are polite and submissive they tread on you. So you have to be strong all the time, although sometimes being assertive often gets classified as being aggressive. They have to give it a name, I suppose. It is a system you cannot beat. Ironically it's hard to get well vest with processes and systems as no one guides you, but pin you down when they feel a need! It feels like a trap all the time-walking on egg shells, never belonging!

Do not get me wrong, work is work, and you will meet with challenges all the time whether from black or white people. Looking for answers, I talk to a number of people both black and white. Trying to get a grasp of this racial discrimination, a friend once said to me that the white people have no chance of accepting non-whites as they have not accepted themselves due to the regime they have been put under for decades by their authorities. He explained that it was a regime, a system that promoted individualism and not communism. After the Second World War, a group of people, mostly Jamaican, got into the ship The *Empire Windrush* to get to the UK. They were clearly not accepted by the majority of British people, but some did socialize with the British women. It was clear at the time that these women were the only ones who were kind. As they went on to marry their black men for love and hide from this regime, they became outcasts and were called "white trash." This stamp promotes the notion that a mixture with black is not desirable. It's worthless. I can therefore appreciate the stress that a child born of such a marriage would face. We see this in our society today. The mixed race child is classified as black, demonstrating the power inherent in those genes. But these children also want to classify themselves above a black person. Most people are not even aware that all human beings have originated from the black race-Black is a dominant Gene! Everyone is trying so hard to run away from the genes that have made them who they are.

I cannot judge as I had grown up among my people, and any race I saw and interacted with was not an issue to me. I grew up in a society that provided stability, acceptance, and a sense of pride in who you are. My mother was the strongest part of that. I realize how much of a challenge I have to instill this in my children, who are growing in an environment with so many racial issues. People say children are "colour blind." Believe me, there is no such thing. You have to love the skin you are in. Besides, it is a desirable skin shade to be dark for so many reasons. I believe that God did not make a mistake when He made me black, so no other human being will get me to think differently. It is almost a bluff that issues of colour have only surfaced to me in England—not even in SA in the nineties when I lived there among whites, some of whom were Boers who instigated racism. It was never an issue. If some did hate me, I was not aware of it, so it did not affect me. It never even made sense really when some of my black friends wondered how I relate to anyone regardless of their ethno-biological origin. I knew discrimination existed, but if I was not coming face to face with it, I was not bothered. Besides, my world is one with every colour, nation, tribe, and ethnicity. My friends and associates were from all ethnicities, and I was content.

In those days of hard-core racism, my friends filled me in regarding the real issues of the apartheid system, which were shocking. But for some reason, I was sheltered from them. Probably my reaction would have been damaging, so God protected me from the obvious. I do recall my reaction when I watched *Sarafina* (a movie based on SA & apartheid); I wondered how people in reality could have been put through such inhumane torture in their own country by foreign imposers.

So much negativism has been placed on "blackness" and what it means to be black by inventors of this ideology, that it became an issue of self-identity and self-worth. It does not go without notice that even among those classified as black people, if there is some chance of a drop of white blood in them, they feel better, even though they are not accepted by the very people they try so hard to belong with. Confusion and the lack of a sense of belonging lead to real disaster to children of a mixed background. Unless a child is strong, understands their origin, and is proud of it, there is bound to be issues. In the nineties while studying in SA, a friend said to me that I was lucky to be black, because I could claim a strong culture. My friend was in the group classified as "coloured." To be honest at that time it did not make any sense to me. I was always removed from the colour mentality. I never even saw her as a "coloured," just a person like me with some differences in skin shades.

Barak Obama shares some of his experiences as a child coming face to face with a need for identity. At a particular school dominated by whites, he spotted another black girl, and as if to deny his own identity, he did not want to go up to this girl even to say hi. He explains how they used to watch each other from a distance in their private pain of inability to acknowledge each other. Even today some black people won't acknowledge each other while trying hard to brush shoulders with whites. Unfortunately, white people are not about to accept them anyway, especially as a collective. Of course those who are human will relate to you as a person, those who do not have colour-coded minds. How pathetic is this? Who is to blame? I have come to a realization that no matter how strong you are, there are walls you may never break.

Another issue of survival I want to highlight is the discrepancies in the social structure. It is the mentality of most people, especially from Third World countries, to believe that there are no extremely poor people in the UK. That is a myth indeed. When I made my dream to come to UK, I made a picture of how I was going to live my life: the type of house or flat I would live in, a lovely area by the sea, and all those fantasies of an excellent living. I have expressed earlier the shock I got when the agency had organized me into a tiny room in a family home. I had never imagined that people could live in such small houses, let alone place me in a box of a room.

With time I began to discover that there are rich people as well as poor in UK. The equity and equality on the list of important issues are not implemented. For a while, I used to wonder why you still find people on the streets begging for money and food when there is such a wonderful social system in place. While there are many reasons some people end up on the streets, there is clearly a difference between classes like in any other country. Though definitions of social class vary, most are linked to factors such as occupation, level of education, and wealth. In the UK, there are about three systems in the social classification structure: upper class, middle, and lower class. However, within these structures there are further classifications such as upper class, upper middle class, middle middle class, and lower middle class.

The general understanding of the upper class denotes the aristocracy and landed gentry, very rich financiers who buy country estates. According to Wikipedia as of 2011, these are normally people who inherit land about three generations from the time at which the money was made. So they are traditionally wealthy, having inherited money and position despite their educational background. I was amazed at one point when a wealthy woman mentioned to me that she did not complete her education. She went on to elaborate that the reason her children are in a private school is to get that which she did not acquire.

The middle class people, according to Wikipedia, are described as those who are in the "middle of the societal hierarchy," "the group of people in a contemporary society, who fall socio-economically between the working professionals and upper class." These people typically have had a good education up to a tertiary level, own a family home, hold a professional or managerial job, and thus earn middle-class salary. Among the middle class you will find professionals, academics, teachers, engineers, nurses, managers, social workers and some middle-level administrators (Wikipedia 2011).

Wikipedia further describes the lower class or "under class" as those with long-term unemployment, pensioners, economic immigrants, and those on state benefits. The majority usually occupy public houses and council estates (a block of flats or an array of terraced houses or ghetto, as we may say). There are many other categories like the skilled working class who hold blue-collar jobs in construction and manufacturing industries or the self-employed. Mostly they hold apprenticeships instead of receiving a university education. There are also the semi-skilled and unskilled working class; they could also hold blue-collar job on lower incomes. They work mainly in car factories, steel mills, and textiles mills. What has resulted in these different infrastructures is a subject not for this book. The writer merely wants to illustrate the social dynamics of the UK society by removing some of the stereotypes or myths she held. This information being taken from Wikipedia is in no way representing a thorough academic research, rather common knowledge.

Chapter Seven
Becoming a British Citizen

You would have thought that my negative experiences in the UK would have thrown out the window the possibility of a long-term stay in the country, let alone thinking about becoming a citizen. My experiences so far did not destroy the inner person that I am, and I do not believe they ever will. In every country, there are laws that govern how the country is run and rules about migrant workers who would like to be citizens. As my children were born in Britain, it was only natural for me to anticipate that I would live in the UK for a long time. At this time, I still held the myth of a wonderful British education that can lead you anywhere. Despite being in the education system and knowing the realities, most of us still strive for British qualifications. The power this resource-rich country holds is not about to fade away. The truth is that even though I identify with people who are disheartened by negative energy, I use negative energy to build a stronger me. Generally, I have not been destroyed by my experience—I won't allow situations or circumstances to break me. It has just been a walk of reality to my biggest surprise. During the peak of apartheid in South Africa, the British people were in the forefront against this regime that simply battered Black, Asian, and coloured people. Some British people even put their lives in danger fighting for the rights of those the regime disadvantaged. The positive aspect of British people does not go unnoticed globally as they embrace humanity with most needed services of survival. Unfortunately they do not seem to embrace the same qualities when you live with them.

Despite all these challenges I have no plans of going back to Africa to stay (at least not in the immediate future). My preparation to become a British citizen was not driven by any negative energy whatsoever. I was simply following my course of life in the UK. Generally people are desperate to be citizens for the added benefits of owning a red passport. The UK, just like USA, remains the most economically strong and stable country. When you travel around the world holding such a passport, you can immediately feel the high horse on which people place you—money is power.

To become a citizen, you have to sit for a test on British citizenship. They want to be sure you know some of the dynamics of the country you want to become a part of for a long time. I am quite laid-back about things, sometimes too much. To finally take the test, two of my good friends were actually behind me pushing me to get rolling. I am thankful to them, because the laws change every time and also the fees increase year by year.

The day I sat for the test, I was rather nervous in case I had not covered all the required elements and faced the possibility of failing the test. It would have been a trauma to retake the test. On that day, I met another white South African who was sitting for the test. We had both passed when they gave us our results. We were screaming in the streets, and to my surprise, we both used expressions that I would have thought only Black South Africans can use (Simunye—meaning we are one). In the UK, everyone begins to face the reality of belonging regardless of skin colour. People are people regardless of the differences; we have same aspirations. And I realized that she actually identified with my having had some bad experiences with the British people. For many, getting a British citizenship stands out as the greatest achievement as it opens many doors, including travelling in Europe without restrictions. I have already mentioned that the English have the power to colonize. A lot of countries that were colonized by Britain still want to claim that British-ness in some form or another. I was educated in the British system in my own country. I was made to believe, even by my own people, that education could only be achieved through knowledge of the English language. It is a true phenomenon that we all look at Western education as the key to success. All the educational books were written in English except for my local language, Sesotho.

It gave me a certain excitement that I would be fully a citizen—whatever this really means as I am equally happy to be an African. I guess more as an opportunity to access an array of things. I knew already that this would pretty much be for the print, not so much for the real practice. We are all aware that this certificate does not work a miracle of belonging—you remain an outsider. I know this as people have lived it, and it will continue. You are born British and only know the culture of the British, and yet you remain an outsider. I was aware of the undercover prejudice, so a legal document was not going to fool me into thinking differently. What mattered was I had reached my goal and became a citizen. In life you have to learn to take advantage of good opportunities for personal and professional development. I see myself as part of the society, educating its future professionals. So the fact that I am not under any border control helps me to relax and do my job to the best of my ability. Of course when you travel the world with the red passport, there aren't many restrictions. This is the evidence of colonial power.

People do all sorts of things to be able to get into the UK, to a promise of a better life. Unfortunately, for many who do not have professional qualifications or high skills that are recognized in the UK, life becomes impossible. When I see how people struggle after leaving good jobs to come to the UK, it pains my heart. The laws are changing every time regarding getting into the UK, let alone to get indefinite stay or become a citizen. My two kids, who were both born in England, often ask me whether they are British or African. I always tell them they are African by origin and British by birth. I am trying to instill in them the pride needed to belong. I already know that it won't take them a lifetime to realize that it is not the red passport that influences belonging. While there is absolutely nothing wrong with being British, I feel sorry for children who clearly want to identify with being British while trying hard to deny their African origins. On this, I can only blame the parents. As a child living in the UK, what else would you know if all your parents or guardians ever did was to tell you nothing good can come out of Africa?

The ceremony for citizenship was more like a funeral than a celebration, not to undermine its intentions. But it was not what I had expected: lively, exciting, and amazing. Well, the English people generally like things done quietly and lack rhythm. It is culturally a norm. A good friend and neighbour had accompanied me to this great ceremony that was to change my life. I thought, "but how?" My life, as it was, needed no more change per se. But it was an accomplishment to finally know I was a citizen. It is some form of illusion that once you obtain your citizenship, all of a sudden you are embraced as one. People remain exactly as they are. You are the one who has to make the choice of how you move forward. The isolation continues as a way of life. The knowledge that I would not be under any border control, even going all over the world, was a ticket to life, but which life? I have no idea.

I did not come out of that ceremony all of a sudden as a new me. I was already engraved in the dynamics of the society, and the way things are would remain the status quo. When anyone sees you anywhere, you are still a foreigner to the general public who do not need to see your certificate of naturalization. To many ignorant minds, there is a belief that being British is a safety net. Research that was done through a BBC poll in 2007 revealed that about more than a third of Asian people agreed that to get on in the UK, they needed to be a "coconut," meaning "brown on the outside but white on the inside." This demonstrates that it is not the paper that will ever make you acceptable in this society. So self-acceptance is the biggest tool for empowerment.

Chapter Eight
Prejudice

Throughout life, people have prejudice of many kinds, whether on colour, character, race, social class, gender, age, ethnicity, disability, religion, or many others. So what is prejudice? From aspect of various writers, this can be described as an attitude (usually negative) or feeling of dislike towards someone or the members of some group based on their membership in that group. Making a prejudgement of the individual or group based on little or no factual information. The roots are from social, emotional and cognitive sources. It often overlaps with discrimination and stereotyping. Making assumptions about others or a situation without adequate knowledge is almost a disease of humans—inherent in our genes. The most prominent form of prejudice is racial discrimination. It is much easier to label, because people see the clear difference in their origins. Oftentimes, one who feels disadvantaged may judge an incident as racially motivated. Due to the wide-world awareness of white dominance, even though white people may face some similar prejudice in Black or Asian communities, it is almost justified as it's assumed they are the ones who tried to dominate the whole world. In other words, they deserve what comes their way. Some of these conclusions are very hard to justify even if they are true because often you cannot prove it. Thus, a lot of institutional racism goes unpunished.

We naturally pass wrong judgements on another person who, in our opinion, does not belong with us. You may have friends across all ethnic groups, and yet a nasty remark may still come up when dealing with someone from another ethnic background or race. Things like, "Oh these Pakis are all over the world!" And yet you have good friends who are of Pakistani origin. I grew up in a country that provided stability, acceptance, and sense of pride in embarrassing the self!. So as it was, I had never really had issues of race or colour. For me, it was always that the world is full of colour and loving it. People may say, "Where were you in the peak of apartheid in SA, that you walked out so clean not touched by its negatives?"

Lesotho, unlike SA, was not directly affected by apartheid even though my people did suffer who lived in SA. A friend made me aware of why my world truly was never colour coded. The white people who lived in Lesotho were mostly American—Peace Corps. They came there with a purpose to serve. They were ordinary people who looked humble. We, as a nation, had our hearts go out to these people, we simply wanted to embrace them and make them part of our lives. So colour became insignificant. I remember as a child we embraced these people. The children we went to school with were always protected by us even at each other's expense. We felt they looked different so we had a duty to make them feel at home—at least as far as I was concerned. Somehow we felt sorry for them, and they were in our country for a good purpose as missionaries. With time, I did realize that these people actually enjoyed a better lifestyle in our country than its own people. They got priority for better housing and health. Looking back, yes, they did do their service but equally compromised the people who believed they came to do a good service. I am not angry about it, but the reality makes me upset. I just want my people to have a fair chance.

No one can take away having tried to be the better person despite what sort of treatment people gave you. Now, I do panic about the sort of experience my children are going through in England. Children are not silly, they are unfortunately aware of these issues in some form or another. You would have hoped that kids would grow up with no stereotypes, but when parents are involved, there is no chance as kids pick these vibes from their homes. It was a beautiful afternoon on wonderfully done cricket grounds. My daughter and I went to watch my son's away cricket match. Being the first people to arrive on the grounds, I mentioned to my daughter how it seemed I was the only mum that day to watch the boys play. Within minutes, mums arrived one after another till there were about five or six of them. The amazing thing was that even though they found me there, none of them said hello. My daughter picked on it, "Mum, is it not funny that none of these women said hello to you?" She went on, "That is why I do not bother to greet these people as they will only ignore you." My heart sank as I then realized that she was already facing the isolation of being in a white society. When you think you are protecting their innocence, it just defeats the purpose. They are made instead to feel their social isolation pretty early. I talked to her a bit more, explaining that in life, you have good people and bad people, the ignorant and the enlightened. It is a choice she would have to make who she would like to be. Equally, that she should not try to force herself on people who have no regard for her. As if it were not enough, after the match

I was talking to the cricket coach for my son when one of these women just barged in, interrupting my conversation since she wanted to speak to the coach. When I made her aware that I was still talking to this guy, she continued talking as if she didn't hear me. I then had to assert my voice for her to get it. She then apologized that she had not seen or been aware that I was talking to this guy. Now this made me rather angry, "I am probably as invisible now as you all ignored me on the grounds where we were all sat," I said. I told her how it didn't matter as I am used to this type of attitude and behaviour every day of my life in this society. When she began to apologize extensively as she felt ashamed, I thought to myself "what a waste of life!" She then felt it was the time for her to stretch her hand to greet me and introduce herself. I did shake her hand—what else are you supposed to do? I am quite a tall, well-structured, and poised woman, so for someone to say they did not see me is quite an understatement. I reflected on how well my son related to all these boys, as he knows nothing else. And yet the parents won't even acknowledge my presence in any way, and for the parents, they are just cheering a black boy who is playing well—nothing else! I am comfortable with who I am; I do not need another person to endorse my self-worth or self-esteem. But we are all human, seeking human recognition and acceptance. I know in life you cannot await people to make the first move, but believe me I know what I am referring to. It is way too tiring—you say hi today; tomorrow they act like they have never seen you. Who wants to put themselves in that kind of continuous stress?

She must have told the other women what I said as the following day during pick up, one of them came to me out of the blue, praising how well my son had played at the cricket match. It is all so shallow and calculated—I cannot even deal with it. Should I regret that I was so embracing of other people? No, it is good to be good even if it does not benefit you or your loved ones immediately. Besides, being colour blind helped me to be a free being. I did not see colour even when I lived among the white people of South Africa, the so-called proper racists—they show it openly, unlike the English who will still fake a smile. My white friends were colour blind, I guess, as we related beyond colour. They were a brother, sister, and friend like any black person in my life.

People in all walks of life suffer some form of unconscious bias towards another person based on the same stereotypes described above (some of which are height, assertiveness, body weight). This happens anywhere, including areas of work where people need to be united to meet the organization's objectives. This unconscious bias emanates from a need to protect oneself—a state of self-protection to prevent people from taking you for granted. In an educational module designed for staff to create awareness on issues of equality and diversity, several scenarios were created to demonstrate these issues of bias. In one of them, a receptionist was awaiting the arrival of a professor, but she missed the actual person due pre-conceived idea that it would be a white male. So when a black male had arrived earlier, he got dismissed. When a white male arrived at the reception asking about the professor, the receptionist was only left with embarrassment. It is unfortunate, but the receptionist, being white herself, did not expect that the professor was black. We come across this kind of bias only too often. In fact, it forms part of our daily existence for those who understand and experience "black taxing." It reminds me only too well how I have been challenged and dismissed even by colleagues who perhaps didn't know me at the time. Unless true education gets instilled in people, and people are willing to open up, "black/minority taxing" will continue. Those who do not feel its sting and the serious impact it has on others will only ignore its reality. In the presentations of the educational tool described above, the guy who was doing the presentations went on to indicate, "Unless as a people we acknowledge unconscious bias, it will continue." When people are aware it means one can compensate and take necessary action. The employers on this issue are looking at it more from the productivity point of view, aware that when people are put in a box, they begin to question their own knowledge which hampers productivity.

My children, on the other hand, are growing up in a very different world, a world that will bring racial challenges throughout their lives. People often say children are "colour blind," but I do not think that they are. They do see people as being of different skin colours or shades and accept it without putting any racial issues on it. It is adults that teach them from their homes, the society at large, about those colours and what they mean. Both my kids at a very early age (five and seven), asked me why the majority of kids in their school were a different colour from them. The interesting thing was that they did not label these children as white, but rather they said some were pink, yellow, peachy, etc. At a time when I did not even think I would be dealing with such, I had to teach them about colour and humanity. How everyone is beautiful as a person not the colour of his or her skin. As if that was not enough, they read a book my daughter had picked from school library about the life of Mandela, his imprisonment due his colour. They were so distressed by it, as they could not understand how another human being can treat the other that way just because they were different. Withholding my own bitterness and knowledge of the depth of this, I had to teach them that human beings can choose to be bad, and how they have to choose in life to be good people, how against all odds they should remove themselves from colour consciousness as much as they should embrace the beautiful skin they are in. My mother never had to deal with such when I was at such an early age of innocence, but I have to walk with them, empowered across all challenges. They need to know who they are, as that balance is power in itself. I have come across a lot of children who end up with no sense of identity as adults, when parents failed to teach them about the foundation of their being. In their inability to accept themselves, they failed to teach their children about accepting the skin they are in.

I still love the diversity and rich heritage you get from being exposed to different people from all walks of life. This is still my life as I see it. Of course I wouldn't impose myself with groups or persons that are obviously colour orientated. There are plenty of these people, and for me, they are the losers really. As a woman of black African origin, I am not a disrespecter of persons in anyway, being from whatever background. I talk to people as I come across them, if they are not willing to engage in a conversation I move on. Believe me these things do happen under your very nose, whether among the lower socioeconomic class or the upper class. Some people actually act it for you to see that they are ignoring you. It is such a funny reality. Watch this, you are at the school for pick-ups or drop offs, and you can see the obvious reality of some snobs or ignorant people avoiding having a conversation with you. It's almost like a conversation or mere greeting will draw them into you, so rather, they ignore you. Or they think that you will ask them to take you home to feed you or ask them to pay your kids school fees. I don't understand it, and I am quite tired of trying. So I do not bother with such people, and many of them are losers. I think of myself as someone with such a rich personality that ignoring me counts as a loss to them. I sound too proud you say, and that's not very professional. Well, it is the truth, as I know it—sorry if you are offended. You do get invited to coffees or lunches, but only one or two people are interested in talking to you. Even the ones you relate well to when not in a crowd barely talk to you. You do have to reach out to people in conversations, too, but hey, it is very demanding and unnatural. So why do I still go to these things? I believe that I am on a journey of life discoveries to learn and to make enough observations to make my conclusions on some solid ground.

A friend, upon discussing these issues, once said that some ignore you due to their own insecurities and fear or lack of knowledge of communicating with people outside of their box. This could be true of anyone, though I have my doubts. For me, it is a colour thing. Coming to England has opened so many wrong doors to reality checks in discrimination, yes even among Black and Asian communities who claim to be disadvantaged in a white-dominated society. My goodness! If you want to learn hard-core racism, it is among the minority groups. Black Caribbean (BC) prejudiced against Black African (BA), Asian from India prejudiced against a Pakistani, mixed race seeking belonging by denying the Black roots etc. It is a crazy world. A friend described it so perfectly when she said it boiled down to slave mentality, a notion that when you are mixed, your hair resembles that of the master so you are of a better category. Oh God! How can you be a better category by resembling someone who enslaved your ancestors—proper brainwashing? A friend shared a painful experience of her relatives in a mixed marriage. The kids due to an identity crisis blamed and resented the black parent for marrying a white person, and they have ended being unacceptable in both groups (not white enough nor black enough). I do believe that the power of parental empowerment about love of self would have been beneficial if done at the very early age. No matter how much we talk about diversity and multiculturalism, the effects of brainwashing will live with us forever unless as humans we all chose differently. There will always be mixed marriages, and there is nothing wrong with them. It is the society that labels things as acceptable or unacceptable.

For decades, the world has managed to portray so much nega-tivism about Africa that it's only natural for ignorant people to con-clude, "Nothing good can come out of the continent." It takes people with brains to know that actually every good thing comes out of Africa. If nothing were good, then the white people would not have tried so hard to own it and take every resource at whatever expense. Timber-lake (1988) identifies some of the real setbacks in Africa's fallen econ-omy. The greed and mismanagement of the African leaders is what has put this beautiful continent where it is today. Prejudice among Black Africans and Caribbeans emanates from ignorance: the Caribbeans think they have a better command of the English language, as that is the only language they know. On the other hand, Black Africans have come to the UK with an educational heritage that most Caribbeans born and bred in England have not taken advantage of, even though education was offered for free. When people are enslaved and believe in their master, they develop a mentality that fails to stretch beyond where they have been placed. False promises of housing and benefits enticed the people, and thus they settled for less. It is therefore not amazing that a lot of the prejudice comes from the non-elite groups. You cannot blame them; that is all they know. Who shall we blame for this appalling ignorance that is weakening the bonds we need as "a people" to conquer the world?

A friend admitted that the BA often labels the BC as uneducated slaves or products of slavery that have no direction. This also stems from barbaric influences or perhaps a tendency for humans to under-mine someone who probably for no good reason has their nose in the air. One of the reasons the BC never took up the opportunity for an education in the UK emanates from the false promise of a better life during the black migration from Jamaica (Sewell). The little they got offered made them comfortable, and they forgot to look at the bigger picture. Those who came from solid families did not just settle for less. In a discussion with my mum, I was in part trying to find answers to slavery and who was to blame. She told me the black people were to blame for having allowed themselves to be enslaved. Genetically, we are physically very strong, but emotionally very weak and easily misled by other people by the promise of something that we do not know or are not exposed to. As a nation, we have no love or unity, the reason the chiefs could easily trade their own into slavery. The unfortunate thing is that even when the slave trade stopped, we continued to blame slavery at the expense of moving forward. We then remained where another person wanted us to remain.

Think about what the Nazis did to the Jews. They took everything from them, even a chance to see another day of success. But at the failure of the complete eradication of their nation, the Jews worked doubly hard to prove they were far better than was believed. Most people will be aware of the history of the Jews in the concentration camps, where they were tortured beyond measure. During the Elizabethan time, the Jews were barred from holding most jobs. They ended up taking jobs like tax collectors and moneylenders at interests. This made them hated even more as the work was classified as immoral and prohibited among the Christians. Look at the world today, it operates from the same system of moneylending with high interests. The Jews are a rich, powerful, and highly successful nation. I am not claiming I really understand the background details of how the Jews ended up getting such treatment—whether they deserved it or not. I only know the surface information or the after of what went on prior to this.

On the other hand, the Black/Asian people, especially from the Caribbean, continued to live as if they were enslaved even though slavery had been abolished. There is however a proportion of successful Black/Asian people in the UK. There is evidence that a higher percentage of success is in the Asian people due to the unity they have as a people. They support each other, succeeding together and not alone. We could equate it to their population being higher than blacks. Look around and you will notice, without fail, that every petrol station, little shop, and phone shop on the high street are run by them. And it's usually the whole family, immediate and extended. They also employ their own people—that's power! Most black people do not work well within families or communities. It is always about who will get better than the other one first. Lack of unity is disruptive in any phase of life and any situation. It does not take a genius to understand why Africa, being such a resource-rich country, is struggling with poverty—monolithic, selfish leaders from top to bottom. All they think of is how they can make themselves rich and invest in the Western world. Of the few who actually love Africa and its people, their voices are not heard.

Fine. You may say the British did not apologize for all their wrongs in the trade. But opening the doors for empowering oneself is another type of acknowledgement for their wrongs. So how can we still blame them for our failure to use opportunities? Do not get me wrong, I share the same sentiments of anger and resentment, but you have to move on. Black/Asian people in UK today, who seem to be making a success of their life, are mainly those from Africa and India, compared to the born and bred from the British Caribbean. It is only an observation; we can go into research later. It appears, therefore, that other unimportant things cloud their lives as they aspire to be or feel better, I can only assume. The educated and exposed have none of these issues. It goes without saying; they have bigger, more important things to fill their day. The Black/Asian Caribbeans who came to the UK were working class (nonprofessionals doing manual labour) who could not get jobs in their country. So they came to the UK to take up menial jobs such as bus driving, cleaning hospitals, and working as auxiliary nurses, or in menial jobs at the councils—all the jobs that the white British did not want to do. The majority of Black Africans came to England to get an education or came to England with professional qualifications. This pattern is still pretty much the same today. Now of course, many people come to England from all over the globe for different reasons, including job opportunities and education. During the time of Idi Amin leadership in Uganda, the Asian people who took flight to the UK, made a success of themselves despite obvious prejudice—they stood together.

In the twenty-first century, there is a greater influx of other Europeans into the UK due to the widening of the European Union. Most of these people do menial jobs and often struggle to live in the UK, as the standards of living are quite high. In the end, some people end up going back to their countries as they find it hard to live in the UK. It is much more of an uphill battle for nonprofessional people, who often live in appalling conditions. And, unfortunately, even professionals who cannot get the jobs they were trained to do end up doing anything available.

It is among the minorities that I learned so much about colour consciousness, skin shades, hair obsessions, and origins. Skin lightening products make big business as both Asians and Blacks use them obsessively. People aspire to have a lighter skin at any cost. The use of long weaves, wigs, or hair extensions never had a negative connotation for me. I believe in exploring with different hairstyles. But realizing that the motive for the majority of people is to attain long flowing hair in an attempt to try and be somebody else made me think again. I think people will continue to live the way they like. The big picture for me is for one to be comfortable in their skin. If you are not happy with yourself, no matter what you do outwardly, it won't resolve the inner issues. In the celebrity lifestyle or to anyone exposed to style and beauty, it doesn't matter whether one is black or white. Everyone experiments with hair extensions, weaves, and wigs for multiple reasons. I have no issues with the use of these devices, and I would not advocate that for us black people to demonstrate we love ourselves we should stop using "fake hair." Our men criticize how we like looking unnatural, and yet many shallow ones do not have respect for their women. There is absolutely nothing wrong with hair exploration if not used to gain self-worth. If it works for you, why not? I have always loved my skin. I never worried about obsessing about the look of my hair or lightening of my face. I am not suggesting that when people use dermatological products for various issues such as hyperpigmentation or melasma it should be an issue. I grew up in a society where anyone could be teased, whether or not you had a lighter or darker skin shade. I never, therefore, felt anyone was superior in any way, regardless of the shade of his or her skin. This wasn't racial as it involved all black children. But now living in a society obsessed by racial discrimination, this only goes so far.

An Asian friend mentioned to me how another Asian did not belong to her class, because she is of a darker shade. Everyone is running away from being dark. What is wrong, really? I love my skin—it would be sad if I didn't, for sure. As a society, we have to realise that beauty is very diverse. An artist, a white, male friend, mentioned to me how he has only ever dated black women. He told me that he found only these women attractive with their amazing features and inner beauty. Of course, every woman takes pride in her looks, whether she has nice long or short, wavy or curly hair or nice skin, whether light or dark. In Africa, hairstyles are very diverse, ranging from short, natural hair, to long, natural hair to woven, braided, or extended hair. You may be surprised, but even being completely bald is a style, complimented by beautiful jewellery. I do not remember anyone being obsessed about hair till my days in a minority community in England. Everyone is striving to look European. The other contrast is how white people admire and envy the diversity of black people's hairstyles. A number will admit how boring their hair is, since they cannot do much with it. The truth is there are people with naturally good hair whether black or white or Asian. The diversity of black hair in England was influenced by the damaging effects of the weather and water. So to keep it up, you have to weave, braid, and wear wigs in some seasons as I began to realize. I have thus explored so much with my hair after a couple of years in England, seeing how damaged my natural hair was. In the minority groups, hair obsession even affects relationships of men and women— amazing. The priority for a black man (who lacks substance) is to marry someone with long blonde hair.

An Asian family will not stop at any juncture to prevent the marriage of their daughter or son to a black man or woman in the understanding that black is not desirable as media portrays. But they feel honored if their child marries a white person. This is still the notion of white superiority that people continue to embrace. Sometimes people who grow up under white oppression believe that marrying a white person means they are accepted by society. That is why I admire the strength of Barack Obama and many strong, balanced people who accept who they are. Amidst all challenges of race, he knew his strength was in finding himself. He needed to embrace something with which he belonged. It is the strength inherent in those genes that have made him as powerful as he is and the strength of that beautiful Michelle. The two of them make perfect sense in my world. For a number of reasons, a lot of us with like minds believe that if Obama had married a white woman, he would not be as strong as he is. I am not dismissing the fact that he had a strong influence of white women in his life (his mum and grand mum).

Let's face it, any drop of black genes is classified as black—that's power as I see it, despite how people use it negatively to belittle others. I am not saying this to make myself superior or to feel better about myself as that alone would show that I have lost the point. Black people have so much strength, enough to survive any pressure. If the tables were turned and the white people were the once enslaved, tied like animals, how many would overcome? It's almost like society has the intention of putting black people under pressure in any situation. But "why" will remain our question till the end of time—whenever that will be. We can only win by continuing to fight—not with physical weapons, but with the continued strength of our voices and actions.

All these make me reflect on one incident in my life when someone that I really loved told me that even though I was the ideal woman, the problem was that I didn't have long hair. I was so naive in relation to such issues, so I took it very lightly and accepted it. He was being honest, though it did take me aback. I mean this guy was the closest thing to my heart at the time as we had developed a really good friendship. I then realized later on that even his mother's negative attitude towards me was because I was black. It just shocked me how any human being can behave so badly, especially when I had done nothing wrong except befriending her son. No, he was not white. Otherwise, the hair thing wouldn't have been an issue. Can you see how damaged we are? It has only come to my awareness that the "coloured" people of SA classified themselves as better than blacks. It is only in their awakening that in the UK we are all classified as coloureds and blacks—I hate that word coloured! What is so "coloured" about my skin? And it beats me that white people say blacks look alike, as we are really distinctly different skin shades—the darker shades of grey, body structure, hair, etc. For me, it's an issue of the white person just dismissing us. They do not care who you are as a person unless you are Oprah,

Obama, or some TV personality. We cannot all be celebrities or big figures in society to claim the same human element of a white peasant. When they see you, you are the same as the other black person they saw along the corridor or by your office desk. I have lived among whites, coloureds, and blacks in SA, and I was never colour conscious. I was never aware that some thought better of themselves over me because I was black. I hung out with everyone regardless of his or her colour. To date, I still have friends across nationalities, ethnicities, and colour. You may think, get a life, but it is pretty much my reality. If I was ever a victim, I was not aware of it, and I will never play a victim in any given situation. One thing I aspire to is to never take bitterness to my future. After all, I am not perfect either. Surely, I have hurt people with or without intent. As someone said, the only way to change the world is to release any feelings of anger and bitterness and resentment toward God. Doing this takes the burden away from you.

Turning to a very open-minded, white, English friend to understand these forms of racial discrimination, she said, "The real discriminator or unconscious prejudice has to do with behaviour, culture, dress, and accent."

In her own words, "The so called Biblical 'shibboleth'—the test you have to pass to get through the gate—the social filter for tribal sounds, voice, and signals. We then pick up signs about 'others' through half-conscious or non-deliberate messages from our parents even before we understand the language."

It is the same prejudice that the Catholics and Protestants used in Ireland. As we continue to want to identify with others that we feel we fit in well with, it gets stronger. We can then either develop or fail to develop, becoming insecure adults. In striving for being accepted so we do not become outcasts, we then formulate unconsciously these prejudices, thus excluding anyone in the group that may awaken our fears.

She disputes my idea of racial prejudice being the most obvious form. It is simply because society can then make laws against this type, we think we can easily control it. Rather, the deepest prejudices we all have to fight against in ourselves from infancy are not to do simply with "race" signified by "colour" or physical signs features. These easy-to-see surface signs are like flags of ="the real differences - which are all the other 'tribal' and cultural behaviours that we experience as soon as we come into contact with 'non-tribe'". Of course, nowadays in the so-called global village, we are learning to take differences in our stride. But it takes a lot of time and a lot of work for us (as cultural groups and as individuals). In another example, as a lecturer, my friend stated that she had seen and heard Chinese students bolstering or justifying their irrational thoughts, opinions, fears, and political indoctrination about Taiwan by saying that Taiwanese students eat strange food and smell funny. Thankfully, she said this was about twenty years ago, and today's students from China are very self-aware and accepting of all cultures, less indoctrinated, and more self-reflective and rational.

So we can say that, in a way, culture equals prejudice—especially if politics is a big ingredient. People who say "I don't talk about politics" are often the most prejudiced and unaware that they are prejudiced and ignorant about the reasons. So education, really thinking about things for yourself, is a big help in fighting prejudice. We have so much education in place already in the UK colleges and universities, where cultural and diversity awareness is the order of the day. But change only really comes to those who embrace and welcome it.

In England and Scotland, the way you speak—even if you are English or British—is a big factor even now. In Scotland, you can have two Scottish parents, but if you were born in England and go back to Scotland with an English accent, there is an immediate (albeit only semiconscious) prejudice from "real" (born and bred there) Scots. So you have to work harder and prove yourself to be likeable or acceptable and then gradually, you become not just "like us" but "one of our own" through your conforming behaviour or by becoming familiar and getting accustomed to the customs or "fitting in." But where colour is an issue, is much more deeper and complex to unpin.

On a trip from Dublin, Ireland, while reaching the Port of Holyhead, the police were doing random checks. When we came near, after looking to see who was in the car, they pulled us aside to confirm details. It was my kids, my friend who is white, and me. When we left them, I asked her whether she thought we were just a random check or it was because I was black. We had a long discussion about it, and the truth is sometimes you will never know the criteria used. But clearly racial prejudice stands out more. Just like me living among the whites of South Africa and not experiencing racial prejudice, there are people in the UK of African and Asian origin who may never have experienced it. The reality is the majority of us in the minority experience this only too often.

There are other realities about racial prejudice that can be taken out of proportion. The sensitivity about white people making racial remarks is quickly taken up in some instances. And it would appear that the same remark from a black person is much more acceptable. It is true that due to the prolonged pressure that black people have faced, it's only legitimate for the remarks. The statement made by Labour MP Diane Abbott in 2012 that "White people love to play divide and rule," is one that makes perfect sense to me and many in my box. However, due to her social standing she was scrutinized for making such "stupid" remark. I do not believe she meant those in an attempt to be racist, only to acknowledge the reality. Uttering any remarks that may be portraying racism have been classified as a crime. In her position she had to be politically correct despite her inner sentiments. It reminded me of an incident at my son's school where a drama teacher had made racial remarks that the boys in that group had picked up on. They were practicing for a school performance, and when some boys suggested they do certain moves, she remarked, "We don't do that as we are not black." It was some ghetto movement implying that only black people are ghetto. Being someone who did not even understand ghetto life, I was not so much offended by the implication of someone being ghetto. But, when my son came home, he told me that when she made this remark all the other boys looked at him and went on to tell him that the teacher was being racist towards him. It made me feel sick. I did not want my son succumbing to these stereotypes. I don't think it meant much to him, and I ensured he did not become negative about it. One of the boys had also told their parents about it, and the parent had approached me with concern. I decided to approach the teacher and reported to the headmaster. Talking to the teacher was for me to clear the air and make sure there were no misunderstandings. I was sure in my heart that the teacher had no issues with my son as a person. But I needed her to learn to be careful what she says as a professional person especially. The unfortunate thing is that she missed my point, as she went on to tell me how she is a Jew and would never be racist. I was so disappointed when she then dismissed me to attend to another parent. I wrote an email to her, to which neither she nor the headmaster ever responded. What would you do if you were in my position? What conclusions would you make? I would have pursued this matter, but I felt so tired. I know my life is a fight forever—not with weapons of course. But indeed, a daily battle against racism in a so-called civilized world.

Chapter Nine
Beauty Is in the Eyes of the Beholder.

Due to the movement of black consciousness, the phrase "black is beautiful" has been in existence for a while now. While I do believe black is beautiful from whatever angle you looking at, I do think deeply about how it came along. Of course, the people, having been under so much pressure and being made to think less of themselves, had to uncover the reality of what is inherent in those wonder genes. It is more about a depth that goes far beyond any physical looks. It is the "humane" found in most people classified in this category. No one under the sun is black or white, but someone came up with a classification that would label people and the connotation that goes with it. Stereotypes, unfortunately, cannot be avoided. White has been portrayed to denote power, authority, and superiority over other groups, revealing deep ignorance. This goes with the power of speech, media, and socialization. Power to conquer and enslave blacks and Asians gained them some superior control over their "slaves," as it were. So, in an attempt for black people to love themselves and identify with blackness, this phrase remains powerful. Even in the normal expression of the English language, "white is beautiful" doesn't sound right. Not that it denotes superiority or makes me feel good, this type of thing—it is the way it is. I have not suffered from insecurities of beauty because of my skin shade. Going back to basics, the human origin is black. You can read a bit more about it, as it is not the subject of this book. Black people are powerful, physically as well as emotionally, to have endured the hardships which only we can bear. Unfortunately did not use this kind of strength for building one another. I know some of us may not agree with it whether we are black or white. If something is much more powerful, stronger than you, you will seek ways to overcome to make yourself better.

I guess as the white people never had to stand and fight against racial forces, there has never been a need to assert themselves even though they suffer privately against other human struggles. The black people went through unnecessary struggles and still do today, so to empower the people was a big thing. You read about stories of powerful men like Dr. Martin Luther King, how they fought hard to empower the people, to shake off the imprints of slavery in their minds. Mandela spent twenty-seven years in prison, fighting human rights for black folk in South Africa under the severe apartheid system. The idea of thinking that there is something wrong with being black has been engraved from the slavery, almost like brainwashing. Someone once said if you grew up being told you are nothing or worthless, somehow that becomes an imprint not easy to shake. So clearly, some brainwashing has taken place for too long, placing people in this unfortunate box. Only the strong can survive. For this reason, we have to teach our children the meaning of beauty.

In the African American community, beauty goes as far as good hair or bad hair. If you have hair that's not kinky, afro-looking, or fleecy, you have good hair so you have a chance in society. My heart only bleeds at these stereotypes and for those who have been affected by their sting. I have watched some of Tyra Banks' shows that explore issues of hair—call me naive, but I couldn't even believe the impact these have within the black community itself. I cannot blame these women for not liking their hair, since they have been brainwashed completely. I have never been critical about the diversity of black hairstyles—it has always been just ways people choose to wear their hair. It is a reality also that hair adds to how women feel about themselves. The only time I was personally challenged about my hair was when it began to be thin due to constant processing, plaiting, and weaving. The versatile hair accessories were no longer a choice, but a must to give my hair a chance to grow. Since I still don't have problems with how black people choose to wear their hair as long as they are not trying to be someone else. I do not use this variety of styles because I am trying to be white, and I will not at any point dispute people's choices to plait, weave, bond or whatever one wishes to do. It's a thing to be done according to one's personality. The exploration with all these sorts of hairstyles happens across all ethnic groups whether celebrities or all those exposed. In fact I believe that what a girl does with their hair is entirely their business. I like what Khosi, wrote in the South African magazine Drum that she edits. She states how she is puzzled by the debate that black hair sparks-if you bought it, then its yours! There is a notion that black people do lots to their hair in an attempt to imitate straight hair. A friend of mine also on discussing hair styles for black women, went on to say he admired black women who keep to natural hair styles, and not all these weaves, wigs, extensions etc. He said how it demonstrates that we have not accepted ourselves. He has his own opinions clearly and I respect his views. In fact I respect a black man who puts real value to black women. However, it's not every black woman who uses vague hair to aspire being white. My hair has nothing to do with being black, or what I may be aspiring. As Seete describes it: hair does not define who you are, what you believe or your cultural norms. If a hair style one maintains makes them happy, then let it be it. It is quite an in thing across all racial groups for the exposed!

For me, beauty has always been "skin deep," as this was instilled very early in life about love of yourself—the skin you are in. Some of the expressions such as, "My black is triumphant. My black is radiant. My black is fierce," express just how skin deep black is. When I look in the mirror, I see a woman who shines from within. There is no doubt that beauty is a relative term, depending on individual judgements. In every race, nation, tribe, and colour, there is a degree of what is classified as beautiful. But really, even today, I still do not see why in Caucasians, being blonde with blue eyes is the desired look. My friends who are Caucasian and fit that category just laugh about it when I ask them to explain this. When you are taught continuously that something is beautiful, you soon begin to believe it. This is the reason why as parents what we say to our children is very important. If you tell your child that they are beautiful, it becomes an eternal mark of victory for their self-worth. Equally, if you pass negative messages to your children, that is what they will believe and dwell on.

When you look around in the media, promotions for beauty products for hair, facials, and body are all given a white person's touch. Well, I guess in England, this is the world of the Caucasians, so other minorities do not matter. But of course people around the world look up to anything that is European as the thing to go for. Look around the world and see how everyone copies the Americans. How we all aspire to reach the "American dream" whether physically or by mimicking the American way of life. Well, this country is powerful, look at the general influence it has around the globe. Their power is felt by individuals, nations, and communities at large.

The notion "black is beautiful" is a movement that black people formed to explain beauty in their own terms, away from the European interpretation of beauty. In a way, it is a part of the struggle to free themselves from the bondages of slavery that perpetuates in different forms. It was an attempt to define beauty in your own world, not in the eye of another person. Most cover girls in magazines are Europeans to dictate how all of us should see beauty as a white phenomenon. The growing cosmetic industry in skin beauty is much more well advertised with white people as most users. If you have a business in this industry, to be successful or well-known, your advertisement should be white dominated, despite the fact that a lot of non-whites today do use cosmetic innovations to enhance beauty. In a *True Hollywood Story*,

Tyra Banks stated how she would continue to encourage the modelling industries to expand their definition of beauty. She had had bad experience due being black in the industry. So you can clearly see how the media influences how we view beauty.

I am very open-minded and try not to judge people by the colour of their skin. I do not mind mixed marriages, but I have an issue in cases where especially the successful, black men pursue a white woman as if to acknowledge that their success is a ticket to get the unreachable white women. I even know some really intelligent guys who feel better about themselves if they feel accepted by white women—it is sad. Do not get me wrong, there are genuine relationships despite skin colour—but every sister will identify with this. The majority of black women today admire men like Barack Obama, who married someone with depth that would identify with his struggles, someone who would share his life in its reality. Indeed, he married the most beautiful, intelligent, well-poised, elegant, confident black woman of our time. It proves that he is comfortable in his skin and embraces his African origins, embraces the strength in those genes! My heart went out to one black, extremely beautiful, intelligent, and educated woman who had come to a conclusion that no man likes her, be he black, Latino, white, or Asian. She broke out in tears in one of Tyra Banks' shows. I thought what on earth has happened to her self-confidence—yes, beauty is really about confidence. Lots of people looking at her dark, glowing skin would die for that skin. But obviously there were some inner issues there.

Consciously or subconsciously, society has put a label on white power to all humanity. So a lot of people, who are not well rounded, aspire to be in a relationship that will help them hide behind their identity to cover their low self-esteem. It's a pity, but such people have taken into the slavery mentality. Some people, despite being intelligent and well achieved, still suffer low self-worth due sometimes to the exposure and damage of racial discrimination. Thus, they strive for acceptance from the very people who rejected them and will continue to reject them. While I wouldn't say I suffer from low self-esteem, I have come across situations where the social isolation based on the colour of my skin has left some mark of the reality of belonging. I believe I am not under anyone's mercy, but as a social being, while you are ignored in a group of people who pretend not to see you, it is off-putting, and can challenge your self-esteem.

Someone I knew well made a comment once that got me thinking about how as people we think of or see each other. He mentioned to me that some of the black girls are so beautiful, he would love to go out with one of them. I realize instantly that for him beauty was colour coded. As I thought deeper about it, I realized that really, when I look at white people, they are just white, and I am not able to read beauty instantly. I am not implying that there aren't beautiful people among the white people. It is simply that as people, how we view or see beauty is determined by our socialization mostly. I have black friends who will only date white men and visa versa. People who are real make their choices based not so much on colour, and thus beauty is individualistic and only shines in the eyes of the beholder.

You cannot deny the beauty of that radiant, smooth, chocolate-brown skin that glows and penetrates deep into your eyes, making you look young and wrinkle free! Thousands of white people today spend so much money to get this dream skin in sunbathing, tanning salons, tanning lotions to give them that sun-kissed look. Amazing isn't it? Some of my friends always complain about how pale they looked and how they wished we could swap skins. It never really made much sense at the time. In the other extreme, some black people use whitening creams to look white only at the expense of damage to their skin. We therefore need to realize that beauty is skin deep. It's about confidence and accepting who you are, and that is how people will accept and love you. People accept you mostly because of your attitude, not your skin colour, when it comes to real human issues. Look at the sad story of the amazing music legend Michael Jackson. His failure to accept the skin he was in led to so much disaster in his life as he went through face changes. He died a really sad man who lost so much of his identity. If you do not love yourself, who will?

Real beauty is measured by confidence. When you are confident, full of glamour and elegance, you do not obsess with the outside beauty. How many people who are physically beautiful with all the features to die for are still unhappy with no self-worth and go unnoticed? Cosmetic industries are filled with people in search of the ultimate looks—nothing wrong with that, but for most of them it is more about how they feel inside. You can buy the looks, tits, teeth, lips, but not glamour! The designer Kinder Aggugini explained glamour as a feeling, or state of mind—feel glamorous and you shall be. Glamour is something you have within that cannot be bought. The passion and wit behind all those looks say it all. Antonio Berardi further explains glamour as that moment when fantasy becomes reality, when time stands still and the memory can continually strike a chord in one's mind. Playwright Arthur Miller once said, "A beautiful woman can turn heads, but real glamour has a deeper pull." Looking at glamour and beauty, it was kick-started by Hollywood in the 1930's. Of course it was white-orientated. No wonder beauty is seen in these eyes!

I believe in the power of the genes inherent in me as a strong, triumphant, confident, black woman, who will stop at nothing to embrace life and achieve her goals. This is pretty much how I see beauty and the glamour. Barack Obama in *Dreams From My father* states that to be black "was to be the beneficiary of a great inheritance, a special destiny of glorious burdens that only we were strong enough to bear." He is a powerful leader of our day, an inspiration to all those who appreciate the depth of beauty and strength!

The beauty, power, and strength of a black woman will never be recognised until a black man recognizes it. This is so true you cannot begin to understand. I hear young black males talking of their ideal woman with flowing blonde hair. You cannot judge people by what they like or do not like, but the unfortunate thing on this matter is the motive or influence of such thinking. Equally, I hear young black women talking of black men as being the wrong colour, so they will not go out with them. You can only feel saddened by the brainwashing that has perpetuated for so long it's almost a norm. If a black person prefers to date a white person, there is nothing wrong with that. There are white people who will only date blacks; it is a choice. For as long as there is humanity on this circumstances, let life be. But if one is going to stop exploring an enriching relationship because the other person has the wrong colour of skin or the hair is not blonde and flowing, it is a sad place to be. I do have high respect for black men who love and respect their women, for people who aspire to succeed together as they embrace the beauty in blackness!

The biggest message is to appreciate yourself or else you become a carbon paper. The truth is if you do not love yourself, even the people you are trying to cling to will think less of you. Most importantly, internal beauty is much deeper. Nothing can get at you in any way as long as you strike that confidence within you. Walk it, and talk it!

Chapter Ten
The Power of Eye Contact

Eyes play an integral role in our lives; they help you to read, view objects, view danger ahead, and see people. They provide an effective communication tool: for the building of good relationships, for romance, and for use in general situations like work. When we look at the dynamics of love and falling in love, the eyes speak volumes even before the spoken words. You will know how someone feels about you by the way they look at you. An expression like "our eyes met, and that said it all," gives a depth of how deeply eyes communicate. When people intentionally avoid giving you eye contact, it makes you feel unseen or unappreciated, as well as unimportant or of less value. Sometimes in a meeting, the person talking may avoid looking at someone they deem scary or intimidating. In her book, *Everything I've Ever Learned about Love*, Garner expresses that love begins with a gaze and that it is over when you can no longer meet each other's eyes. Have you noticed how babies look continually at their mothers? It is a depth of communication only eyes can express.

Culturally, eye contact has some implications, too. In my culture, a younger person may not look directly into an older person's eyes as that is a sign of disrespect. In other cultures, giving eye contact denotes being attentive. Excluding the minor discrepancies, eye contact can help one get a job and improve one's self esteem. Depending on the situation, it can be inviting, deep, soulful, or expressive.

When more than two people hold a conversation, the one talking will have their eyes fixed on the person they value or believe needs acknowledgement. Of course, people who are well rounded and generally confident about themselves will give attention by eye contact to everyone in the group to ensure the interest of all parties. While these tendencies of paying more attention to a particular person by eye contact happens to all groups of people regardless of colour, I have seen how in a group of people you get easily ignored or not seen due to devaluing you as a black minority. Only when they know you and what you have achieved are you acknowledged, even then it depends on many factors. It happens even among your colleagues, people who have the same academic background or position. So for me, it is simply that they chose not to see you unless in a one-on-one situation.

A group of students came to me once, expressing how they appreciated that I try to keep eye contact with the whole class. Of course, this is easier in smaller groups of about twenty students. In a big lecture hall of about two hundred students, it is not easy. As a person, I am cautious of not intentionally ignoring another person in a group. You can think about how you would feel if people ignored you in a group. It's not worth it trying too hard for acknowledgement. Believe me, I have experienced this in the society of the British people. It is not funny, and it is based on colour more than anything else, in my opinion. Even those who have regard for you as a person, as soon as they see another white person, their eye contact goes to them despite the fact that you would already have been in the conversation.

For good presentation skills, presentation consultants would agree that good eye contact is essential as it cuts physical distance, helping communication on a personal level. This also demonstrates participation of the audience. People try to make eye contact with people on whom they want to make an impact to win their respect. You keep eye contact with someone to acknowledge the significance of that person. Eye contact across ethnicities boils down to prejudice as discussed in chapter eight. The saddest truth is that majority of ignorant, uninformed black people will ignore another black in seeking through eye contact approval from the white person in a group. The slave mentality has gone too far. A lot of people reading this know exactly what I am referring to. In a society of white dominance, you would have hoped that the black people would look out for each other. Ignorance goes such a long way; we need leaders who can educate the society.

I recall a number of instances involving work-related issues where someone deliberately chose to avoid eye contact as measure of disregard. A friend shared an experience of being assigned specific patients as a doctor, and yet during a ward round the consultant literally chose not to ask her opinion about certain issues of care, rather sought by eye contact the opinion of another white person. We see it, feel it, all the time in every walk.

Chapter Eleven
The British People

Anyone living or who has lived in Britain is aware of how isolating the culture of the English people is, isolating, lonely, and not understood by its own people. It's all about a personal space that should not be invaded by any means and extreme politeness, which sometimes loses its meaning in a society that is now so multicultural. In my first year in England, I went back home after a couple of months for holidays. I was in a supermarket doing some shopping, and I could not help but notice the carefree nature of shoppers, how no one cared if they came too close to you and bumped onto your trolley. It was a common understanding that where there is a crowd you are likely to bump into someone. In the UK, there is a lot of "Excuse me. Sorry. Please," in attempt to keep away from each other. While to some extent this is good as a tool for respect for one another, it has its negative impact on people that are so uptight. People almost avoid talking to each other due to fear of the other person's response, or they are so used to personal space that they reject attention even if it would take them away from misery of loneliness.

Apparently, this is a Southern way of life. I am told, for example, that in Scotland people are much friendlier with each other as a society. I was in a shop in my earlier days and began to talk to an old woman who was shopping with her cat in Marks & Spencer. She told me she was buying food for Betty, and I discovered Betty was her cat. In my culture, animals do not share similar names with people in order to mark the difference. She lived alone with this cat, and I began to feel extreme sadness for her. What amazed me is that she acknowledged being lonely and yet admitted how she wouldn't want anyone coming to her house. In Africa, they would have thought she was a witch not to allow visits and a chance for communication.

I had a neighbour once who, due to ill health, had to retire early. As a highly educated and achieved person, she would not accept help at any cost from her social services contact even though she could do with the help. She told me she would rather be found dead in her house than accept help. While it is good to be independent, I realized just how deeply isolating the culture is.

There are surely positives to the social isolation and personal space that people in the UK practice. Sometimes being too much into people can get on their nerves. I guess as long as there is a balance in this, it would be ok. The lifestyle is different, determining how people relate. In the UK you can be so consumed with work and your personal routine such as taking care of kids, work, or study, that weeks and months can go by before you have a chance to ring or pop in to someone's house. In fact, it is not a norm for people to just knock on your door. To visit someone, you have to make a prior arrangement quite in advance. It is partly cultural but also the fact that life is at a different pace. People also live in different towns and cities, so if you drive a long way to see a friend and they are not at home, it is a waste of time and money. But even when living at a close distance, it is a norm to ring first.

After a while you adapt, and it becomes a normal way of life. For me, it gives me a proper balance to know I have certain friends that can just pop around my house with no prior notice, and that I can do the same, no matter how busy I am. Part of being me and being human is the social interaction with people. You may conclude I am a needy attention seeker. Oh no, quite far from it. I do enjoy my own company without feeling lonely. But I like to share ideas and life with others. I love people, because they make me who I am. As people, we share our joys, sorrows, our ups, and our downs. All this provides an opportunity for growth, individually and collectively. When I watch British movies and see the strength inherent in the characters playing different parts, portraying the challenges of friendships and relationships, I stop and wonder why this richness of character is not portrayed in the day-to-day life of this nation. Maybe it is only shared behind closed doors. I see so much superficiality in the British people even in their kindest gestures. Maybe they are superficial against nonwhites, but I do not know. Does anyone out there have an answer? Somebody tell me where do I get these ideas? Most of my friends who have British friends will say the same thing. Is it the cultural differences? You often hear people say, "Oh well, she is my friend, but at the end of the day, she is white, so you are never sure what's next."

I share these sentiments and am still seeking an explanation to them. Maybe the white people also think the same of us. All I know is the "white" person will only trust the opinion of another "white" person regardless of the vagueness of the opinion—strength in unity. The irony of it is that even if you are an expert in a particular area, you still get ignored till you have worked extra hard to prove a point.

The ability to manipulate the world through colonization has made them powerful over others. Thus the world believes they have something that other countries do not have and can only be found in the UK. Let's face it, the riches we now see in the UK were built out of the resources they got elsewhere, like Africa. Well, who can blame them? My mother would often say that if you allow another man to manipulate you and take over your very life, you are playing the foolish one and will therefore suffer the bitter consequences. She maintains that enslaved Africans have no one but themselves to blame!

English is an international language, and you are deemed elite if you speak it. They were clever; they ensured that wherever they went in the world, there wouldn't be a barrier such as language. This barrier would prevent them from achieving their goals of using and manipulating the locals to get what they want.

British people are good at using space. Look at the houses we have in the UK, a small island with almost seventy million people. You begin to understand the structure of terraced, semi-detached, town houses, and flats. They have managed to save a lot of land by constructing these types of buildings. Of course, you still have the rich with acres of land. When I first visited England in 1996, I was extremely disappointed with the nature of things, the old, rugged-looking buildings. I didn't understand the terraced houses, the semi-detached structures. I did not see the streets of gold I thought I would find. Now, I have learned to appreciate the phrase "Do not judge the book by its cover." I was impressed by how the inside looked impressive despite the outside.

They took the idea of the slavery game from the Portuguese, but the British used it for their benefit. They changed the names of the people of African and Asian origin they enslaved to keep their culture, and that is a symbol of power. Most training schools were changed to adapt the British system. Without realizing it, people had succumbed to their culture in the name of education. Later, they opted for democracy to free the slaves. I still recall the pride I had knowing that my "O" level (General Certificate of Secondary Education or GCSE) examinations were marked or prepared by Cambridge University. I felt that we had the best education system in the world. We still have the same British system in my country today, even though the British have left it. They use something, and when it no longer serves an intended purpose, they leave it. Look how they brought Christianity to Africa to manipulate their way so they could get the best out of the people and the land. You are in the UK, and realize that Christianity is a thing of the past for most of them. They have managed to colonize so many countries in the name of education—that's power!

But talk about disaster relief such as for famine, floods, earthquakes, and hurricanes worldwide, and the British people will be there offering their undivided support. There are so many charities run in the UK that support other countries. They are an absolute virtue. Some people may say they are only paying back the world what they owe and that all this is done through manipulative diplomacy. Tolerance of other people is evident as seen by number of asylum structures in housing, accommodating millions of people seeking refuge from all over the globe. It is funny though that, yes, they agree to house those seeking help and then just ignore them once they have offered the material gain. It is in the UK where the huge bulk of asylum seekers are housed. They may not like you, but they will tolerate you enough to give you the superficial support, and of course, this gains them worldwide recognition.

If I could take anything from the UK to Africa, it would be the work ethic. With the exception of lazy people who just want to depend on our taxes, they have an amazing work ethic regardless of the type of work one is doing. The commitment and energy they put into work is commendable. If a road needs fixing, they will work tirelessly, even in the night hours, to ensure the deadline is met. I was talking to a friend, and we reflected on some instances in relation to work in Africa. In a small village where a tarred road connected the villages into a nearby town, the men working on this particular road would be on that road for months with little evidence of what they have been doing. The funny thing was that every time you drove past it was tea time, lunchtime, or break time, as they were always standing and talking or eating. Believe me, this is pretty much how it works out there. In the UK, work is work regardless of whether you drive a bus, sweep the streets, or work as a chef. As a lecturer, I am aware of my input to student learning both in classroom teaching, student contact, and the number of hours, and I must say we do give our very best to students, even if they may think differently.

On a larger scale, they stand out as advocates for human rights. The legal system is written in such a way that no one may be compromised on legal grounds. But the same system still fails the minority communities. It is quite complex and complicated.

They may hate you, but if you ask for directions or information about something, they will go out of their way to ensure you are very clear about the issue in question. The motto "The Customer Comes First," is utilized to the best of their ability. When you go to any shop, restaurant, or car service stations, you receive the best care. They are aware that customer care keeps the business going. Of course, you still meet the odd, ignorant people who fail to meet customer care based on colour. You begin to wonder what the colour of money really is. There are areas where white people still look strangely at black people. Oh yes, the same people who make laws against discrimination still practice it.

Someone might begin to think that on a personal level I do not regard well any white British person. On the contrary, I have met complete angels in this same society, those who have gone out of their own comfort zone to meet my needs. People who have offered me the kind of support I cannot quantify. You will always have someone in your corner no matter how blurry everything seems. This support has come from my work colleagues, parents I meet at school, and in the general walk of life. When you are a full-time, professional woman, holding a full time job, life comes with a full package of challenges. Couple that with being a mother of young children who need your full attention, with no family around you, it is all uphill. A lot of women do it, so I do not want to give an impression of self-pity. When people ask, "How do you do it?" The answer is always, "I have no idea, but I keep going!"

While most people look forward to school holidays, it is not the same for me. I have the added stress of organizing activities for the kids either in camps or with child minders. So, to say the least, the support I have gotten from individuals is immeasurable. A person will come to me out of the blue and say, "I will take your kids for so many days, as I know you work." Another person will give me information about which camps are available. Yet another will say, "Drop your child every day at my house, as I am home for a period," which may make weeks at times. I always say angels come in so many forms, and for me, I thrive because there are people willing to extend their hand when I most need it. I do hope I give others with different needs support when they need it, too.

Believe me in the busy, isolated, British society, when someone just offers to pick your child up from school, it takes away some stress from your fully packed day. I will not stop singing the praises of these people with their special touch on my life regardless of their race. I remember once I was completely trashed from work and going through a rough patch of being a single mum. Someone had picked one of the kids for a play day. I was making my way to her house to pick up my son with my daughter after picking her from school. As we sat down to our lovely tea, I continued to feel extremely exhausted with my head spinning all over the place. This poor woman, realizing I wasn't myself, ended up taking care of my kids and me along with her own. It was a complete nightmare, as I needed to sleep for a while, or else I do not know how I would have made it home. When she offered that we should all sleep over at her house, I reassured her that I would be fine. I felt at that level it would have been asking for too much. I just prayed that I would reach home safely that night, and I did.

Sometimes, some of the isolation comes from the nature of one's work. A lot of the mums I know do not work, at least not full-time like me. So even with good intentions of organizing play days and outings, I hardly attend since I am busy. Some people may begin to think you are just not interested, so they stop including you in things that may appear as you being left out. But it is too much work to try and keep up with these people I do not blame anyone in cases of that nature, because I would not want to appear as the needy one who must be thought of. I want to be in a position to organize social events, but, presently, I am simply living my reality with just enough room for my immediate life.

People are complex though; you will never really get a full grasp of their intentions. As nice as they may be, they still try to treat you like a stranger in some situations. You can only maximize the positive aspect and swallow some of the negative vibes at times. It's almost like performing a service to humanity—I helped you when you needed help, but really we do not belong together. I have already mentioned that the same people will ignore you at some point. I have no full understanding of why they do it and continue to do it.

Chapter Twelve
Friendships and Relationships

In all human socialization, interactions between people lead to relationships of some kind. As people relate to each other, they build relationships with those who share similar interests. We all relate well with people who share our sentiments, while we learn from other diverse groups who may not view life in the same manner. My mother provided that first friendship as the greatest psychologist, friend, and builder of hearts. Unlike me, my mother is reserved, and yet she has helped to embrace, cherish and understand the value of other people in my life. When my father died, she lost part of her life, because they had a great, though a short life together as mentioned in earlier chapters. Even though I remained the major and most important being my mum focused on in all aspects, she has supported her family amazingly, as well as many people unrelated to her in that biological sense. I learned, therefore, quite early in life the extent of human relationships.

I love people, as a matter of fact, and am a bit naive in stepping carefully till I get burned. That's life. I guess you have to live and learn. She had figured it out early enough to be a mum as well as a friend without jeopardizing her parenting skills. This has shaped my life positively as I knew I could talk to her about anything. Believe me, I used to get a hiding when necessary, as she did not confuse friendship with discipline. She helped me to be a well-balanced child through her guidance; she made me aware that it is good to have friendships across the board, boys and girls alike. She learned to remove herself from stereotypes of the people in her circle and time—the cultural issues. So yes, among my best friends growing up was the boy next door—he hates his name now that he is older, so I will not use it. We'll call him Thabo.

When visiting my home, one of my uncles, to show his disapproval of this boy, was on my case big time one day after he left our house. I was in high school as a boarder and had come home for holidays. My mum had a small shop, and we had stayed all afternoon in this shop (doing work of course). I was extremely upset and told her when she got home. This was the first time I saw my mum disagree strongly with her brother, and a lesson was learned. She went on about how children are children and should be left at that. Believe me, my mother was very strict with discipline before you have any ideas. Thabo and I were such best buddies, that everyone in that small town thought we were soul mates. We had a lot in common, and we understood each other, but I knew he was like a brother, even though he thought differently when we were at university. He was such a poet, no wonder he went into literature. I know he has written a book or play or something like that. But when he got married, the relationship took a different turn, as you can appreciate. Besides, the girl was quite stuck up. Obviously, we kept our distance but were happy when we bumped into each other. I still hold him dear to my heart today even though we have lost contact for a long time. In my opinion, friends should remain friends regardless of whether married or not. If you are a trustworthy person, you should be comfortable around any person regardless of their sex. But many people have issues about it due to what sometimes happens. The reason, I believe, depends on the person and not the circumstances. Of course, you do have to respect people. If your friends or acquaintances do not feel comfortable with you being alone with their spouse, move away. It tells a lot about the person and the insecurities they have with their spouse. I have had and still have friends with couples and singles alike. I truly have no problem. You cannot blame people for being insecure, and I am not suggesting one has to pursue relationships that make one party feel compromised. You cannot call someone a friend who does not trust you. Respect for people should take precedent I guess, but life is too short to hang around people who give you negative vibes regardless of their origin. Yes, even people you have total trust in will disappoint you big time. I guess that's why we should always leave room for disappointments where humans are involved.

The notion that "a friend sticks closer than a brother" is often used by many of us. It is much deeper than the words. As an only child, I haven't known the love or friendship between siblings except with my cousins that grow up in my household and a wider family circle of love. I do not recall struggles between us because we were only together mostly during school holidays as I was away at boarding school. I believe my mother always tried to ensure I related with other people so as I wouldn't be a selfish, isolated child. So indeed, I have enjoyed rich, deep relationships with people both within my family and outside. The presence of other people in my life has moulded me into who I am. I do not dwell on the negative impact of people because it would not carry me anywhere. There is a reason why some people do not need to be in your life. Some people are more mature than others or it may be that we all simply look at things in different ways. There are people you can trust fully, and they will always be in your life even just in memory. You learn so much from other people. You learn how to deal with disappointments and move on. Some friends may not even live near you anymore, but when you meet you still have that strong connection and move on in your talks as though there has not been any break. I guess people's fundamental character does not change with time. It's only experiences that teach you new heights in relating to others.

My friends are my family, a strong support system in my daily challenges of life. One writer, Kathy Lette, describes your girlfriends as being like your "wonder bras, uplifting and supportive." She also says, "You need your friends as an outlet or else all your anxieties would simply be soothed by burying your face on a pillow for few hours and screaming and steaming." Of course I am referring to great minds, and great thinking, those that share your sentiments, realists who make sense of their own lives and the world around them. Not those spiritually constipated people with empty minds who dwell in so much negativity as they go around judging everyone instead of examining their own lives. Believe me I know such people only too well. For many people who are negative, judgemental, and generally clueless, it emanates from feelings of envy and resentment of other people who are positive and getting on with life.

I am not so naive about friendships. Even though you may have who you see as wonderful friends, they are the ones who have an ability to destroy you in one form or another. They may start to feel jealous of you for whatever reason and thus say things to bring you down. While there is nothing wrong in fully trusting people, they can use that to destroy you. I believe that at the end of the day the one who trusts isn't on the losing end. What do you have in life, if you have no trust? The big question is are there true friends on earth? The answer is yes. If you are a true friend, then there are true people out there. Many times even those people who may find themselves in a position where they have said negative things about you, it doesn't necessarily make them bad people. People have inadequacies that make them empty and thus fill the gap by trying to bring others down. It is a gamble in life that is unnecessary. As people, we all talk about one another in one form or the other, but when you feel the need to destroy others, it is at this point where we all need to learn constructive discussions.

Some people are in your life to feed on something or the other. When they are aware of a situation of distress, they will be there to feed on your news. But you soon realize that because you have the strength they wish for, they begin to stay aloof, while deep inside, they are destroyed by a complex mixture of insecurities they have in their lives. You can only feel sorry for such people. Other friends in awakening to some form of successes may cut you off as though you would take their achievements away. As people, we are weird and complex in ways that are incomprehensible. I am no angel, so I judge situations as I observe and follow my instincts. There are things that happen with friends that even trying to unpin them will only leave you with confusion. You therefore have to learn to let go of certain friendships even at serious costs. Overcoming situations where broken friendships were deep can be tricky. It plays on your mind even though you may know it's better to leave things as they are. Some people do not know how to leave room for disappointment, especially where trust issues are challenged. This is when the true nature of people surface and the demarcation between friends and family. You can simply walk away from friends, but with family, there is an obligation, a responsibility. So no matter what happens, you will need to resolve issues.

As I was growing up, most people would comment that I was ever protective of friends. This is not the case; my issue is to stand for what is right, regardless of who is involved, family or friend. I defend facts, not the persons involved. Unfortunately, some people in my walk of life have misinterpreted this analogy as just defending people I love. For me true love, true friendship is being accepting of the person and being able to point out the wrongs tactfully, so that you don't bring negative energy that was not intended. It goes with maturity. In friendship you have to be able to bring the whole of yourself to the table with your weaknesses and strengths and be accepting of another. In life, we all have to be mindful that what is wrong in your opinion may not necessarily be wrong in the opinion of another person. So step cautiously so as not to destroy with intent. You may, for instance, caution a friend about something with good intentions, but they instead take it as you being a criticizing person.

Life, unfortunately, does not come with a formula. You learn as you go along. How can I claim to be a true friend, or true person for that matter, if I will watch someone getting destroyed and not come to their defence? People are different, and sometimes I wonder how much of these differences should be allowed in life. For instance, is there an acceptable way of dealing with issues? Surely, there should be to some level a scale of normality in terms of people's behaviour and attitudes. Some people hold a view that there is nothing normal under the sun. The norms and values are designed by other people to force them to have the same outlook in life.

There will always be true friends as well as false friends—I do fail to understand the latter. It's either you are a friend or not. We have to acknowledge that different people play different roles in one's life. Some relationships are superficial, while others are deep. You have to choose with whom you go deep. There are people you can go to a certain level of depth with despite the risks—life is a risk anyway! Unfortunately, these are the only people who have an ability to hurt and destroy you.

Back in the days in university, I recall a friend saying to me how I go around smiling with everybody, thinking everybody loves me. I was taken aback really, but after some thought I knew that she was the one with a problem, and I should just move on with my life. Probably I irritated her with my carefree approach to life. No matter how good anyone under the sun is, people will always have something negative to say. We all experience it. Should that stop us from enjoying life? Definitely not, or else you will share the misery of the very people who are negative. Clothe yourself with positive-thinking people, people who boost your self-worth and make sense in your world.

I really believe I have favour with God as He has always made a provision for good relationships with people wherever I have been. Well, I did not have a blissful marriage. Unfortunately, it ended as it started. So you might wonder whether God was on my side then. I believe in every relationship you meet challenges that shape you into who you are no matter how hard it is. So yes, God's favour has never left me at any stage of my life. I have only been led to learn from my mistakes and grow. People have taken me as a sister or friend across all ethnic groups. I said in the earlier chapters, my world has never been defined by colour and I still wish it to remain that way despite the realities I now face. I never thought of praying for favour as the Psalm 5:12 says, "The Lord blesses the righteous and surrounds them with a shield of favour" (NIV 2010). It was only upon reading Joyce Meyer's writings in her book *Be Your Best* that I came across this and thought deeply about it.

Your friends are the sorts of people that define your best potential. Do not hang around the wrong kind of people who are full of negativism and ever charging you with negative energy no matter what you do. Your friends should provide a healthy environment. "If you are close friends with people who are lazy, undisciplined, critical, and have no dreams, they will rub off on you" (Osteen). Definitely, you are bound for disaster if you hang around negative people and will slowly begin to see life through their eyes, unless you are a very strong person, rising above all odds and trying to share your strength. One has to learn and accept that you cannot change people.

People who are negative never really change, depending on their background, socialization, upbringing, and so on. Yes, some friendships you have to walk away from if you want to stay healthy and focused. As Joel Osteen puts it: "your destiny is not tied to people who walk away from you or you walk away from, it is simply that the season for that relationship is over." It can be extremely hard to deal with the reality of broken friendships, especially when you thought it had so much depth and would not be easily broken. However, you begin to realize that some people you have to love from a distance or else they will drag you down and destroy your confidence. Good friends are a source of strength in your trials. They share your lows and highs. They do not rejoice when you fail but encourage you to press on. They are not jealous of your achievements, because they are stable, rounded people. When you build on one another's strengths, they know the best measure of success is to "measure you against you," as stated by Noel Edmonds in his inspiring writings, *Positively Happy: Cosmic Ways to Change Your Life*. So common sense will teach you that people who are constantly comparing themselves with you and are unhappy with your achievements are not worth your time, so move away!

You have to try and strike a balance in friendships or relationships of any kind. It is in relating to others that we learn about ourselves as seen through their eyes. You learn to acknowledge your own shortcomings; you learn to stretch yourself beyond your own selfish way of looking at things. I moved myself away from someone that I deemed a really good friend. Thinking about it today, I feel disappointed in myself for doing that, because I never gave her a reason for why I moved away. We had good times and laughter. We shared some personal stories. In as much as she was such a good person, I had noticed in a number of situations that she still had some colour-coded relationships. In a number of ways, she had demonstrated valuing my opinion only within the confines of the two of us. She would not acknowledge publicly when necessary that the idea came from me. Probably she thought of me as inferior to her, proving stereotypes of racial issues, as she was white. I decided that I was not going to have that in my life—that she was either a friend or not. To date, she still wonders why I detached myself. I believe I should have risen above this and just move with the flow. Because of those racial boundaries she unintentionally portrayed, I felt a deep betrayal on a human level. I still share friendships with white people on a deeper level and have not come to questioning the bases of those relationships. It shouldn't matter what colour skin you have to be a friend to whomever.

England taught me to see things differently. I am not implying that I have found disappointments only in friends from a different racial group. People will disappoint you regardless of their origin, and I have disappointed people, too. I am only reflecting on the colour-coded implications I never knew existed. In the peak of apartheid in South Africa, among my best friends were white people who I believe were not colour coded. They were like a brother or sister, like any blood relation. I am sure that when they read my book, they will be intrigued by my experiences of reality. At the time when I had gone through all these experiences, I was tempted to ask them whether they had racial issues. But thought better not as it would have been inappropriate.

But I did question myself and looked for clues when we met after the experiences I had in the UK. They still came across as the same people I had loved and known for the longest time, the same people that, at the peak of apartheid, I ran to first to express my anger on the system when for the first time I watched *Sarafina*. I expressed how angry I felt and how bitter towards the white people I felt. They looked at each other and laughed, since I had not thought of them as white. We, of course, spoke about it, and they expressed the same sentiments about the regime that belittled another human being.

Chapter Thirteen
The Church

History tells me that the great pioneers of Christianity who came to Africa and India were from England. They came to preach the message of love and peace to all, thus a lot of people were converted to Christianity. But funny, they were given new English names to consider them fully Christians. I have never been critical about why we had to get a second name. My people, Basotho, already had a form of belief in Molimo (God) and had a form of prayer to Him. They understood that the wonders of creation have a higher power that put the pieces together. In their very nature they are known as the most peaceful people in Africa. The national motto "Khotso, Pula and Nala" (peace, rain and prosperity) describes it all. It is a land that anyone was guaranteed to walk about anywhere without fear. Of course, although it remains relatively peaceful, things have changed as every country has its rascals.

While the message of Christianity was good for the soul, the people were made to change their own way of life as they adopted the Western culture as a form of religion. As Mbon, cited in Brown's *An Incredible Journey: From Religion to Liberation* states, "Africans borrow, for instance, foreign politician and economic schemes, foreign academic programs, foreign religious modes of worship, alien criteria for judging what is right and what is wrong." He goes on to say that they "even borrow alien ethics" and that this "kind of uncritical borrowing" has led many African countries to what Joseph Kenny has called "identity fluctuations." In other words, what is coming from outside is much more practiced even though it may not work for its people. But what is the reason for this manner of doing things? If you allow someone to colonize you, you begin to develop the mentality of copying your master. It is so sad to note that such a potentially able country with highly intelligent people, is failing to develop rightly due to these ideologies. The leaders, on the other hand, enjoy using foreign ideas for their own benefits and not for the good of the society that has placed them in that authority of power.

Thinking about it now, it was definitely wrong for the evangelists to totally discard the people's culture, regarding it as heathen. If a certain manner of doing things is not against God's will and not destructive to humanity, who is man to tell another man how to best live his life? I love God and have a personal relationship with Him as a Saviour who loves us just as we are. He is a God of decency, structure, order— He created a very orderly universe, no doubt. Some practices I believe had to go that would not be in accordance with God's way of things. But clearly, people used their human power to manipulate people into thinking of God in their own understanding. Brown explains that in his observations, all major religions demonstrate ethnicity and cultural roots. So people want to paint an image of God or a deity that looks like them to create a feeling of belonging. All my life I have never questioned the colour of God as I deemed other things took precedent or were far more important than colour. However, look at the deeper picture of black people's experiences, for the sake of peace, they never questioned the intentions of the missionaries who brought the message about Christ Jesus and presented Him as white. I can see why in the long run they began to question some things. And why they began to make their own image of God.

I read a book that implied that Jesus was white. I began to ponder on the pictured representations from artists of Jesus as a white person. Over time, people got tired or rather disillusioned with foreign ideas of a white Jesus and came up with notions such as a black Jesus. I understand their frustrations from the distorted picture of God as I understand Him. When I think of my Maker, I do not think in terms of colour, but rather character. This, in my understanding, is how as a people we ought to embrace the nature of God. In a way bringing a physical picture brings all sorts of images, almost like worshipping an idol. The Bible urges us not to make any images of God lest we fall exactly where we are today with an image of a white Jesus denoting God. Sometimes I do wonder whether it is beneficial to question everything around us on a physical as well as spiritual level. God has made human beings a little more intelligent than the other living creatures. So we might therefore argue that not to question is folly. I guess that is where faith comes in, for things that are of a spiritual nature and are hard for humans to understand. I am comfortable with faith as it makes absolute sense to me. I am not in any way implying that one should not question certain practices even within the church where they worship. When people are not comfortable and unsure why they practice in a particular manner, especially if it's not backed up by scripture, then they begin to place the one who questions as not being full of the spirit. How ironic!

What took me by surprise was the reality that the country that had pioneered Christianity had now moved away from such a belief system. I can only speculate that sometimes when one achieves material success, unless standing on a solid ground of what they believe, they begin to see power as being from the self. I was so shocked to realize that most churches have been abandoned or converted into pubs, houses, or flats. It took me a while to marry the reality that what I always deemed as structure for worship and praises to the Maker was nothing but any place where people may recite or maintain some sort of business. I have always appreciated, respected, a building constructed as a church, Synagogue, temple, or any other name we give to places set aside for worship. This emanates from what I was used to as a child, the family ritual of a formal structure of worship. Now, I have a much wider understanding of what church really is, people who come together to worship with a common purpose. Church is not the structure, but the people who make it. I still like and embrace the idea of a special place of worship as it provides a sense of a haven of peace no matter the intentions of some people in it. It is a social structure of people who share a common goal, somewhere to go for fellowship.

This is not a judgement, but an observation. As a people, black people are quite receptive in accepting and accommodating new ways of life or beliefs without much question. The humane inherent in our genes harmonizes humanity. But due to all the things that the black people have encountered on their journey of challenges, someone had to begin questioning the way of things, tired of the analogy of portraying a white Jesus and yet not living up to the standards of the acclaimed deity.

Observations and questions arise about how it is possible that the same people who took blacks for slavery were claiming a God of love and a Jesus who saves lives. In the slavery market in Ghana, there was a synagogue that after people were tied up worse than animals, their slave masters will go and pray. What do you call that? Tony Sewell, in his book *Keep on Moving: The Windrush Legacy—The Black Experience in Britain from 1948*, describes how the white man has used religion—Christianity in Africa, India, Jamaica (once they had dumped the people there)—to dominate the indigenous people in the ideology of religion. Every cultural practice was classified as heathen, including their form of worship and praise to the Maker. So everybody had to mimic the Western way of worship to be accepted as a Christian. This kind of mentality has contributed to adoption of a Western culture. Brown has stated through his careful observation that all major religions are ethnically and culturally rooted. So when a person adapts a particular religion, he or she adapts a particular form of worship that is representative of its ethnobiological origins. It is not surprising therefore that Christianity represents Jesus as white, which is quite contrary to the teachings of the Bible. Most Christians, including me, have not questioned much of the portrait of Jesus painting by Michelangelo, who was commissioned to draw a picture of Jesus. We learn from history that this familiar picture we see everywhere today was indeed a picture of his uncle. Like someone said, when Jesus came on earth to represent God in the human form, we read that He was of the original Arab, indicating he was of a dark skin. If Jesus was born in Lesotho for instance, and I was an artist, I would have drawn his picture to represent my people. But as the Bible says; no one has seen God and lived (Exodus 33:20). So intentionally, God did not want us making any images of Him to avoid the same disaster of trying to colour code Him!

Even today, people are still holding onto Christian worship in the Western mentality, myself included as you do get used to things. To be honest, I am not particularly bothered by the obsessions of trying to figure out God's colour, because I know who I am and where I am going. All that matters is that we were made in God's likeness. In as much as I share the sentiments of people who got disheartened with so much misrepresentation of God, I would not advocate for a Black God or any colour for that matter. It would not make me any different to try and prove a point to those who desperately want God to be white. In other words, I would just be like them and forget the main focus of my spirituality and relationship with God. It's when people get indoctrinated without insight that it is sad.

There is nothing wrong with the pure Christian message of love, grace, mercy, and goodness. Also, you cannot ignore the reality that it is the same people who claimed the message of love that supported the worst separatism in the church. In the peak of apartheid in South Africa, the church joined in and used the same world standards of separatism. In South Africa even today, there are still white and black churches–you just wonder which God it is we are claiming to love when we cannot love each other as human beings. When some friends told me that as students at a university in SA, they went to a church that was close by, and one member came to direct them to where the nearest black church was. I was sick in my stomach, and I was waiting for someone to make the mistake of telling me something of that sort. It did not happen, probably God saved me from losing my cool, as I would not under any circumstances succumb to such treatment. In the UK, most churches are now full of black people, meaning Asians, mixed race, or so called people of colour. Why? Is it because most white people have left Christianity for whatever reason?

It is therefore not surprising that with time, people became upset with this mentality of white Christianity. They began to praise a God they identified with, trying to come out of their naive shells of receptiveness. They began to make portraits of a black Jesus. There is a nativity play that purely represents this. There is definitely nothing wrong with such in my opinion. There is a reason why people go to extreme measures to make their voice heard. I appreciate the statement Keith Brown made in his book *An Incredible Journey: From Religion to Liberation* that when people are unable to see God in their own physical image, they will never be able to see their image as being part of God's, though I am not the kind of person who promotes blackness or whiteness. In such matters, we have to take what is good and forget about queries of a negative nature that won't benefit anyone. I love being a Christian. For me, it's a way of life that makes sense. But by all means, I avoid being a legalistic person who only sees the negative in others. I prefer a relationship-based Christianity, where being judgemental is not the order of the day. Too many of us today are so consumed by the outward appearance of people and make judgements based on that.

A story is told of a young woman who in seeking God, went to a church nearby, only to find to her disbelief unkind people. One woman pulled her aside to tell her she should not come to church wearing her trousers, jewellery, or make up. Do you think this poor young woman came back to church? Surely, there is modesty in dressing, but not at the cost of pointing fingers at others. So often and unfortunately, the church is full of people who actually do not even understand the nature of God. These people are thus very quick at passing judgements on others just to prove how empty they are. Some people may take it as a measure of being spiritually weak if you are dressed in the manner described above. Have you come across those highly religious fanatics who will stop at nothing to pin people down? I love God, because He is not like that; He loves every one of us as sinful as we are (not to stay in sin of course).

As people we all learn from others. Upon talking to a friend once, I mentioned that he was much more spiritual than me, that we therefore may not look at things in the same manner. He challenged me that no one but God can determine one's spirituality, that as human beings, we use external things to place people in a certain level of spiritual growth. Indeed, the fact that you are the first to arrive at church, you are an elder, a pastor, a Sabbath school leader, or in any position in Church has nothing to do with spiritual growth. I was quite surprised in a pleasant manner by the maturity manifested in the answer that this brother gave. I had thought as someone with so much depth knowledge of scripture, he would take the same position of people who believe they are standing high spiritually. I must admit I was much humbled and encouraged that there are still people who understand God's nature.

Church means different things to different people. Some see it as the actual building, some as a special place where God dwells, and for some as a chance for fellowship with others. For me, church is not really the structure, it is more a gathering of people who want to share life experiences and build each other up on God's teachings. I could be in my home with my family and friends, worshipping together as well as having fellowship—great! As I was brought up attending church, I do like going for the blessings I get through special worship, songs of praise, and fellowship with fellow brethren. I do know for a fact as well that it is not the church attendance that gains you a relationship with God. I do gain blessings, although sometimes there can be struggles that may not uplift you. Well, that is the way of the world, so you cannot quit every now and then. I do not endeavour to judge people's Christianity by how much they go or not go to church. There are standards to be maintained even in any organization so do not read me wrong. Church does give me a sense of belonging to a people with similar interests and goals. You still find all sorts of people in church—good as well as bad. When I was still naive and excited about Christianity, I used to think it was all about loving, caring, and being considerate of each other's differences. Oh no, if Christianity is not a matter of the heart, then racists, judgemental individuals, and hypocrites, are still there, even holding important positions.

It is in church that people fight each other as brethren on really trivial matters. Why should you be so restless and judgemental just because sister X came to church not conforming to your standards of what a Christian should look like? That time you could have used to listen to the preacher and improve your own life. Or why don't you befriend her just like Jesus would have done? We use so much of our human sentiments in church, we even forget the very nature of God we are on about. Probably I have become quite controversial about certain things that I probably need to rethink. We need to be more concerned about people's welfare than outward appearances. I do believe in modesty, simplicity, and all that. But I equally do not see anything wrong with elegance, glamour in your dress code, and dressing to your best in the house of God. When people go to certain occasions, they dress well, so why not when you go to church? Whom are we trying to fool? In fact one of the most stylish Christian women with extreme elegance is Joyce Meyer, and she is my role model. If God is blessing you, even materially, you have to live up to it as long as you are not selfish. People tend to misinterpret enjoying their wealth with being materially obsessed. Why therefore are we praying for wealth? Of course, wealth without inner peace is worthless.

It is quite unfortunate, but it is in church that people may be destroyed by the leaders when they most need the support. This will not change, because they leaders believe they are executing God's way. I am sure there could be better strategies of discipline where needed, such as dealing with young people's issues of pregnancy out of wedlock, for example. In my opinion, we all know right and wrong, so by the time one is being put out of church for any issue that the church deems as necessary to exercise their disciplinary measures, the person has already dealt with the issue at hand with God. I am not encouraging misbehaviour, but I take it that church should be an extension of parenting, a family that supports both the weak and strong alike. You would not throw your child out of your house for being pregnant or any other kind of behaviour. If you do so, it is at a very costly price of losing your child or destroying your relationship for life. Did Jesus not spend his life on earth relating and showing us the best way to healthy relationships?

In Jesus' time, there was no structural organization, and Jesus encouraged love for one another. He always pointed people toward looking into themselves before another person. Once you have a structure, organizing it so it can run smoothly, problems begin. People then lose focus as they fight for positions, putting determining factors around to who should hold certain positions or who should be dis-fellowshipped. Did Jesus use these strategies? Not at all! Remember the story of a woman caught in adultery brought for his judgement and condemnation? What did He do? He asked the accusers to throw the first stone at her if they believed they were without blemish. Of course, they all left one by one when they realized they were even worse than her. So why can't the church learn and apply these simply principles? It is unfortunate that religious organizations, in their view, do not make any mistakes, since God cannot make mistakes (Brown, K.M.). They cannot think outside of this box, and thus continue to control people at the expense of liberty, and freedom to serve God. Have you heard someone being more worried about what the church will think about a situation instead of God? People fail to make healthy decisions that could impact their lives because they are more concerned about being judged by the church. If it were God we approached first, we will be filled with humbleness not fear, because His nature is love and understanding.

People will always have excuses for doing this or the other, including why they do not want anything to do with church or religious leaders. What is the problem? A lot of us walk a very dark road of spiritualism without understanding God and His intentions for our lives. That is the biggest problem of organized religion, which Jesus did not advocate. You form a structure and immediately, there is bound to be organizational rules to run it. Unfortunately, good intentions soon become the politics that brings disunity and a battlefield of disharmony. It soon begins to boil down to who built the church and formed it into an organization and how the voices of the founders have to be heard. We claim that church is there to provide a common ground for everyone who wishes to worship and fellowship with others. Unfortunately, with all this strife, the practicality of a united people with one goal to love and serve others soon goes out the window. The rules begin to be the centre of focus, and people forget about God. The motto is "How can we punish and destroy the souls of these people who have chosen to be part of this organization?" We all know wrong and right, but even to date, I have not understood how stopping someone from participating in church activities will win them over to a loving God, whatever the case maybe. Unfortunately, leaders are very quick to jump to conclusions and rush decisions that impact other people negatively. The execution of these rushed decisions by the leaders emanates from their belief that they are carrying out Christian duties as God instructed them to. In issues like this, you have to just ask the Lord of mercy to forgive them and continue to teach them human relationship dynamics.

If we ever stopped and thought about how Jesus would deal with any one of us with our faults, none of the ways churches tend to deal with their disciples would be applied. If the person involved has no in-depth knowledge of God, they will cease to come to church for good. No one has a God-given right to judge or punish another or even attempt to determine the spiritual level or status of another person. God alone knows each individual person's faults. Only He knows us.

Experience indeed is the best teacher. While I have shared the same sentiments of the negatives of organized religion, I came face to face with being judged by elders when I flew a relationship that nearly destroyed my whole being. They simply listened to a false story and came to tell me what they thought despite expressing that I was not in a position to discuss such issues. And most unfortunately, the executors of such believe they are doing what God requires of them as their Christian duty in their naivety. You just have to forgive them as they truly do not know that which they are doing. More of this storyline will be on some next writings I hope to publish someday.

Do not get me wrong. Church is not the building, but the individuals that make it. In it you find all sorts of people—those who have grown spiritually and those who are permanently in the dark despite claiming God's name the loudest. I may be judgemental as well by stating this. It is humanity! People just lack vision and are not aware of the value of relationship-focused Christianity that Jesus practiced. So they force their beliefs on you whether you want to hear them or not. Why? Because they believe they are highly spiritual and are in the right all the time. God forgive us all.

Brown has stated that in the mainstream, religion exists for the good of mankind, for providing good deeds, and showing love and kindness to all, but unfortunately, it has done the opposite as continues to be used as a destructive force. The misguided extremists and spiritually constipated fanatics use religion to destroy others, including individuals and masses of people. Do not get me wrong. Some of these people who use religion to destroy others think or believe they are doing their rightful duty to tell others what is right at whatever expense. God forgive the ignorant. Thank God that He is not like us humans. He seeks to understand and love us no matter what.

Once at university in South Africa, my friends were concerned that I did no studying on Saturdays as I went to church and had activities that occupied the day. They said to me that if I were concerned that the church would judge me, they would keep it a secret that I was studying on that day. While I understood their genuine concern, what was striking was the fact that they knew I would be judged by the church and not by God. It did not occur to them that it was a choice to have that time to connect with God and gain the blessings from fellowship with others. I did explain to them to allay their anxiety. It is rather disturbing that in general church brings negativism in people's minds. People will always remember the bad they see or have experienced and thus may fail to remember the original intentions of the church.

What is church to you?

Chapter Fourteen
My Role Models and People with an Impact on My Life

Rolemodel.net describes their mission as promoting the idea that within each of us, there is an ability to inspire those around us by living a life that is more outward focused. They describe that by being selfless we can make the world a better place. People often say, "Live by example," or "Practice what you preach," for in that way you are more likely to have a positive impact on people. As we know it, you can claim or preach about love how ever many times, but if you have little to show for it, people will only criticize you. People are touched by the life you have in relating to others rather than the empty words one makes. Role models are people who possess the qualities that we would like to have and motivate us to want to be better. If you want to be a role model, you have to prove those qualities that make you one. Be an inspiration by doing your very best at whatever you do, be it a teacher, doctor, parent, coach, or artist. It is amazing how people are watching you whether you are aware of it or not.

A lot of people have had an impact on my life: family, friends, acquaintances, colleagues, people in church, community builders, etc. I must admit that without being biased, I wish I inherited my mother's patience, tolerance, and the soft, calm nature she has. For every child that grows in a healthy home environment with loving parents or guardians, the children aspire to be like them. Her influence has made me look at life in a more relaxed manner. To many who know her or have come across her in life, she is simply a sweetheart with a pretty much golden heart. She is the quietest person you can come across, and yet the strength of her character is immeasurable. She is slow to jump to conclusions about anything even if I am involved in it. She seeks to understand why something happened and how it can best be resolved. She maintains objectivity in situations rather than use subjective measures. There are times when I would tell her that a particular friend was being unreasonable and not proving to be a good friend. You will not hear her say, "Forget about them and move on." Now, that is strength! I could go on and on. I guess that's the reason that if she told me to forget about something, she knows it is not worth my energy and is being very objective.

If I singled out any friend by name, it might prove unfair to those not mentioned, but my friends have influenced how I see the world in different ways. Even as a child, I have always had many friends with diverse minds, and each one has a special place in my life. Some friends will be closer to you on certain level whether far or near. You look at your friends and think, wow! I like how that girl runs her achievements, her approach to life, and I think that's exactly how I want to live my life.

People who are very open-minded, strong, principled, realistic, motivated, energetic and living life to the fullest with a positive attitude intrigue me! It is people I meet in the daily walk of life and some high-profile people who have made a global impact in one form or another. They include, among others, Mandela, Oprah, Queen Latifah, Joyce Meyer, Michelle and Barack Obama (as a model family of strength). Only God knows how a man like Mandela survived in prison for so long simply trying to fight for justice. He is an inspiration to many worldwide, both black and white people alike. No wonder that, as a hero, people classified him as Jesus. I think his manner of conduct, of embracing and forgiving the same people who put him in jail without a reason, made people classify him closely to the Man who came on earth to show us the way. It is highly commendable—a definite leader, hero, and a child of God. Oprah, as a figure of a successful black woman, intrigues me in many ways. I do hope to meet her in person one day. Queen Latifah is another figure of success inspiring to black people. I love Joyce Meyer for her connectivity with God, a powerful preacher who, in my opinion, is also very open-minded. Her manner of dress signifies class, beauty, eloquence, and proves that being a Christian does not mean you should live a low-class life. When I look at Michelle and Barack, I see the strength of love, beauty, substance, and a picture of the life I wish I had. We all learn so much from other people, especially when we are open to such positive influences.

From school, I admired my teachers and my tutors and lecturers at university. My admiration of their achievements, of their conduct with students, made me want to make it in life. I also admire my friends, acquaintances, those closer to my heart, and simply those who understand the world as I do. I have never really found difficulties in relating to anyone. I have a vibrant nature, and, like someone once said, "an infectious smile," so I blend in easily. But believe me, I have faced the same intense isolation at times of being in a society that does not see me. People who ignore you and are determined not to notice you despite whatever connections bring you just a bit too close. At a school picnic, I chose to go and sit in a group with others, because someone I always talked to was sitting with them. I noticed that some of the women ignored any conversation with me. I felt the deepest isolation as my journey continued. In cases like this, it is very difficult to then get up and go. I felt that if I left, they would know I couldn't handle it. So I stayed and continued to write my story. Some of the women there, I swear, had never greeted me nor acknowledged my greeting to them. I cannot begin to even understand how people who take this position in life live their lives. I thought about how scary it would be for me if, even for a day, I changed into these kinds of people who are colour coded. Under no circumstances would I want to be this person, because the one thing I believe is not to succumb to such low-class mentality. I am a human being first before any description of skin colour, and to be honest, I love who I am. I guess if I didn't, then I would be in really big trouble!

I admire strong women, who want to make a success of their lives, those who make positive, life-changing decisions in matters that free them from any form of slavery, whether from an abusive spouse, unhealthy social contacts, or dealing with an unreasonable manager.

Chapter Fifteen
Staying Upbeat Despite Challenges

The challenges I have gained so far in my walk of life (not only in the UK) have shaped me positively. In the earlier days of a deeper relationship and understanding of God, I loved to listen to and sing a song entitled "It Is the Trials that Make You Whole." I forgot who wrote it. I understood this in its simplest meaning. That it is when faced with tough times that the meaning of your faith is strengthened, and you become the better, stronger you. It is the time when God comes through for you that you experience His touch, love, and protection. Unfortunately for some people, it is the turbulences in their life that may make them angry with God, as they do not understand where He is when they suffer so unnecessarily. They blame God and lose the vision of His working power in their lives. It's only human to be discouraged and begin to doubt how a God of love and mercy can let you go through heartaches, especially when you know you do not deserve such. Unfortunately, life is like that. It does not matter whether you believe in God or not, you go through challenges just the same. What matters is where your hope is in all this and how you view God.

The expression "I am strong when I am weak" explains the power of God taking control of your life even at your weakest moments. It may be the loss of a dear person, a broken relationship, a serious illness, or any deep sorrow one may be going through. It may even be facing racial discrimination at work or any place. When I was face to face with the challenges at work from both management and students as highlighted in the previous chapters, I could have been discouraged and quit. Quitting has never been an answer in my life. The reality is when you dwell on the negative impact of the experience you are facing at the time or your sorrow, no matter how legitimate it is, it has a negative impact on you, and you may fail to carry on with day-to-day routine.

In life, there is a time for everything: to mourn, smile, eat, and die (Ecclesiastes). So yes, mourn when you have to, but do not linger on it for too long. I do find strength in keeping my head up with a smile even when I know I am torn apart inside. Wallowing in self-pity, defeated, and blaming other people for whatever stress you face does not bear any fruit. Of course, you do not have to like your circumstances. Even though a situation makes you uncomfortable, empty, or low in spirit, you cannot allow such to get you down (Osteen). We have to learn to deal with our situation and move on, as there is more to life than what we have already experienced.

I love life and want to be on the brighter side of it. Therefore, if I stayed negative and felt sorry for myself, it would in essence, be me quitting living my life to the fullest. It is imperative therefore not to let disappointments or negative pressures become the centre of our lives. When I went through turbulence due to a relationship that failed to grow in the right direction, I kept my head up, as that was the only way I knew how to overcome. I constantly talked to God and my close friends and family, and that helped me as I faced my crucible. I did not hide and run away from the reality. Believe me, just like any other person who faces these things, it was an uphill battle, and like we say, "It is never over till it's over!" But I knew that in the depths of it, self-pity or staying negatively in that relationship was not a solution. I prayed for strength to go through the situation with a good attitude, because more than anything else, I would not want anything to steal my joy, the peace I strive for so much. I knew that I would not know how to get on with life if I had no joy.

I kept getting on with life and no one at work even knew that I was going through hell. I had to keep up with my work, had to maintain the same attitude with colleague and students; it was the only way I knew how. When I finally told those in management who, at the time, needed to know, they were surprised. With concern the person involved commented how strong they thought I was, and how she would never have suspected anything. I know it is God who gave me the strength to face my reality. One of my friends said, "It's only strength that one can go ahead and face this reality." How many wallow in stressful relationships due to the fear of going through all the stages of a broken life? It only keeps breaking if you stay in it, knowing it will never fulfil you.

Like we say, life is too short, so you cannot spend it using negative energy. When the going is really tough, count your blessings, meaning you have to look at all the positive things that life has offered so far. You are still alive. That is a testimony in itself. Except for my making wrong choices at some points in life, God has always blessed my life. I am healthy, I have two healthy children, and my mum is still alive and strong despite her physical aches here and there. I have my family who love me greatly. I am surrounded by loving people wherever I go. You have to teach yourself to concentrate your energy on a positive outlook, not dwelling on people who hate your guts. Despite challenges, I have a profession—a good career that has offered me a good job, and I have energy to face the future in its uncertainties. Besides, I believe that God is higher than anything that we come across. The song "Hold on my child, joy comes in the morning, the darkest hour just means dawn is just in sight weeping only last for the night, has been taken from Psalms 30:4-5 helps me to focus.

It is true that each one of us experiences the reality in our lives differently. If someone is crying because they have lost their fingernail, we cannot belittle what they are going through, since for them it is a great pain. What each of us is going through is relative to our terms. Once I went on about how embarrassing my nails were and how I needed a pedicure to someone who was going through a real, life-threatening situation. She was scared for her life and son due to a situation that made her flee a relationship. She said, "It's okay for people like you, with the type of money you have, to be worried about such petty things. Right now I am worried about where my next meal will come from." I immediately realized how as people we carry heavy burdens and just keep on going. I turned this into her being stronger than she thinks, how she should keep pressing on. Of course, I provided practical help. We learn every day. Even though I mentioned my need for nail attention, I was not being selfish. It was just my reality, and yes, that taught me something else. Identifying with someone's situation does not mean you then have to carry him or her on your back as that won't be a constructive manner of resolving long-term problems. You know the saying, "Teach a man how to catch fish, then he will have plenty for life," makes perfect sense as you would have provided a long-term life strategy for survival.

In her book *The Positive Woman*, Gael Lindenfield explains the concepts of a basic philosophy. She understands that women who think and act positively even when the cards seem stacked against them have that great philosophy of life. Among the characteristics of positive thinkers are the progressive, optimistic, sensible, independent, trusting, versatile, and encouraging attributes. I do believe that to stay upbeat you need to possess some of these hallmarks. Applied positively in your life, these can bring out the best you.

My close friends and family believe I am too trusting and am often disappointed. In life, as you relate to people as individuals or a collective, what do you have if not trust? I do not think disappointments are based on how much you trust or do not trust—they come anyway. I guess it boils down to the fact that I have sound values and trust myself enough to transfer them into trusting others, unless there is proof I should not trust someone. When you apply trust to your life, it is natural to expect trust back. If, however, it does not happen, you cannot waste your energy thinking about how not to be trusting. There are people who will never trust you no matter what you do, so move on. Be happy with who you are. I always think that most people are good and that you have to give them the benefit of the doubt. I am not advocating foolishness in dealing with your life or throwing yourself into situations that are appalling, where you know deep in your heart you should not trust certain behaviours in people.

When you are disappointed by people you trusted, it can be very hard. But there is more to life than trying to figure out why someone you trusted said things of a destructive nature behind your back. People are people. We have to learn and live. My philosophy has always been to clarify misunderstandings with people at an early stage to avoid ill feelings. But as you go through life, you realize there are some things you need not follow up on even though they may change the direction of your relationship with someone. No matter what comes your way-stay upbeat as only then you can spread your wings!

Chapter Sixteen
Living to Your Full Potential

Life is full of ups and downs whether you live in a resource-rich country or a poor country. We all face human challenges regardless of the skin we are in. In any society, you find people who have simply given up on life for whatever reason. People go through hell and back and either give up the will to face tomorrow or get up and go. As a people, we use different coping strategies to overcome life issues. Some have strong mechanisms of coping, whereas others have weak strategies. It's a way of life. But the decision of how you choose to live your life rests on you. Imagine if we all moped about feeling sorry for ourselves because the British want to isolate us, forgetting the country is strong and surviving because we are using our skills to empower and educate its people.

You can choose to be happy or stay frustrated, worried, and simply miserable. What you will get, therefore, is what you actually put in in most cases. Every person in my box can write volumes upon volumes of the appalling and unnecessary stress we face based on ethnicity and the colour of our skin. And yet, many of us have used the negatives to build our lives positively. Do not get me wrong. There are people who come across calamities of a nature they cannot understand, as they are actually striving for a happy life. You eat as healthy as you can and yet get struck by a deadly cancer. You pray three times a day for God's protection over your life and that of your loved ones, and yet your child dies from a tragic accident or disease. Grieve when you have to, but you need to move out of that stage or you will have no energy to face the challenges ahead. When my grandmother died, my mum lost her will to go on. She almost lost her soul, and we were all aware that she could die any time during this grieving period. I had to aggressively help her snap out of it. As she knew my love for her, she wouldn't interpret my actions as those of someone who did not care what she was going through. I counselled her with help from a friend who was a professional counsellor. I had to make her understand that though she was going through so much pain, she needed to think of me and my children and those who love her. I even told her I would not forgive her if she died, because she would have chosen that path. We talk about it today and she admits that it was the bravest thing for me to do. It can be done, but you need the support of people who understand your pain.

You cannot blame a system that has failed you as a human being and stay in that state, hoping someone will feel a need to come to you and apologize to make you feel better. In a discussion with a friend, we were reflecting on the power of colonization in Africa from the British people. How they implemented their systems in our countries to make their lives comfortable. They set up a British education, setting up Cambridge GCSE or "O" level as we say, it has since been changed to COSC, meaning Cambridge Over Seas Certificate. This does not get you straight into a university in the UK. You still have to complete the IB programme (International Baccalaureate). In the British system, we were taught and read books that had nothing to do with our immediate environments. The concepts were so foreign that we had no direct connection with them. And yet, we were happy to go for it. I am not implying that it is wrong to read outside your own comfort zone. I read stories of Shakespeare (*Twelve Night, Romeo and Juliet, Macbeth*, etc) with only seeing the scenery through my imagination. While I truly enjoyed the English that Shakespeare used, a lot of the kids had not the slightest clue and were bored stiff by such teaching. Except learning Sesotho grammar (the local language), we were not offered the privilege of learning about our own country in depth or the things that were real to us. What baffles me is the fact that even today, we are still holding onto the system that the British left long ago. Gaining independence in 1966, it is a long enough period to have developed a system that is home owned. I have not researched much into the present education system in Lesotho. But I discovered it was only in 2000 that free education was implemented in Lesotho, a good step indeed, even though it is only at the primary level. The country is still continuing with the British system, not working with local needs—should we then still continue to blame the British? They left our country to develop it to the needs of the society, but what are we doing?

I reflect upon how, as students, we learned the pathologies of so many diseases that, unless one left the country, we would never come across. But, on the other hand, the British are teaching their students about diseases that they will actually come across. In the pathophysiology module I teach, we maximize time on the most prevalent conditions affecting the people of Britain. At first I thought it was patchy teaching, but I began to see the relevance. I still embrace the depth of the education back in my country of origin. If only the emphasis could be around the realities that the nation faces.

I tend to be quite spontaneous in my reaction to things. I sometimes take people by surprise, I guess. A friend, knowing I was going through a hard time, asked me how I was over a telephone conversation. With all excitement, I said, "Perfect," and I actually meant it, though not in the sense that my life was perfect in any way. She understood me even though I still went on to explain what I really meant. Generally I approach life happily and try not to let the perils of life get me down. I am so scared of being unhappy, frustrated, or worried about stuff that I always ask God to take care of things I cannot change. I continually remind myself that it is the bright side of things that I want to put my energy into. Besides, peace is not necessarily the absence of troubles. You can go through the most challenging situations but stay above the storm. So even though the British isolated, ignored, disregarded, and undermined me and those in my box, it's not worth my misery. In the same society, I have found real angels (in many colours), people who have given me real support when I most needed it, whether at work or in my social life.

A pastor who was known to wear a smile at all times describes a situation where he was interviewed by the media in a rather sarcastic manner and how he took it upon himself to remain happy with a smile anyway. They were mockingly calling him Pastor "Smiley." When people are threatened by your contagious, happy self, they will use strategies to pull you down. Be yourself at any given time. Oh how can I be happy, I have so many enemies, people do not like me, you say? If you think people dislike you and you dwell on it, it will soon be a self-fulfilling prophesy. What you dwell on, in time, you become. It is natural to want to be liked, but if it is not happening, move on. Do not appear needy to people as this will make you vulnerable to them, and they will begin to take you for granted. People can be wonderful creatures the majority of times, giving you support where it's due. But the reality is that people get tired of hearing about your problems, how miserable you are, and that you cannot move on because someone else has damaged you. While you may be going through real strife, dwelling on it will only make a misery of you. That is why I believe it is healthy to have a wide circle of friends and relations with other people. When in your assessment, you think person A is getting tired of your stories, you can then talk to person B about something completely different. In the group of friendships or relations you have, you will pretty much know what kind of information you can divulge to whom. Some people are eager to hear your story for the wrong reasons. They want to be in a position where they can then go around with your story maliciously.

Someone I know was going through a really rough patch as we do sometimes. She kept everything to herself due to the fear of talking to someone and the likelihood of that person spreading the news around town. While it is healthy sometimes to keep our dirty laundry, it might be equally damaging when there is no outlet. Talking issues out to someone you trust or a professional counsellor is therapeutic. My philosophy on such issues is if I confide in someone as a confidante and they decide to spread the news around, that person is a loser. I would have healed my soul in talking through the issues. The fact that they will go around in whispers won't change who I am, so be it. In life, someone may try to destroy your reputation, but your character will remain.

It is not that as people we get immune to gossip. It affects us deeply in different ways. The strength therefore is to move on and let people talk anyway. Is it not ironic that you may be someone who strives to see the best in people, and yet people seem to only want to slice you negatively? Should you be depressed and sit at the corner? Oh, no! Be good anyway. Some of my close friends and family tell me I am so painfully sterile in the issues of life. And how unfortunately people I have trusted use this naivety to get at me. I am not sure whether this is a weakness or a strength. But I know that trusting people does not always bring beneficial results. I am not silly or daft, but I know I operate on the principles of trusting till proven otherwise. I have been able to recover from disappointments from people I trust, so let life be.

I am definitely living to my best potential in this very country that disregards my presence in one form or other. Another interesting observation is being assertive to avoid abuse of any kind. When you are assertive and trying hard to protect your self-worth, this is classified as being aggressive. So can we really win? No, this is the reason you should always live to your fullest potential.

Chapter Seventeen
Overcoming the
Common Human Mistakes

Let's face it, at some point in our lives in one form or another we have faced things like jealousy, bitterness, anger, resentfulness, the inability to forgive, feelings of inferiority, etc. Defining jealousy and the negative impact it has on the one crippled by it is the first thing to consider. What does it mean to be jealous? The list can go on and on, envying someone because they have what you don't have: a nice body, house, job, car, an expensive style of living, etc. When you are feeling this way unfortunately you become the sufferer, filled with the uncomfortable emotions of humiliation, bitterness, anger, and the lack of inner peace. You spend so much of your time with negative emotions, trying to figure out how you can catch up with so and so. It is ridiculous! I think it is a real problem that needs attention. I know people who cannot help but stress themselves by measuring their success against others instead of their own goals. It must be a really painful position to be in, and unless the person has insight and owns up to this emotion, it makes it harder to overcome it and perpetuates for the rest of their lives. Why spend eternity in misery, unable to enjoy the little you have? Some people may even express this as having an "I don't care" attitude, when indeed it's killing them inside. With comments like, "Why is Palesa buying another big house with only two kids—it is such a show off," the truth is they wish they were in a position to do that.

No man is an island, and we all aspire to have the good things that our friends or acquaintances possess. People inspire you and direct your energy in a certain direction and there is definitely no harm in that, but you have to watch your motive in getting there. Jealousy does get in the way of relationships. You can't relax and enjoy other people's company if all you do is think about how you can achieve what they have and more. Psychologists suggest you speak to a friend about it, even if they are the ones you feel envious towards. It helps to clear the air, I guess. You are facing your demons and more likely to get resolution, if you want to change that is. Sometimes people who envy you—your persona, position in society, the fact that you are strong, unbreakable—may even use emotional blackmail to control you. It is aimed at pulling you down to their level, in that way you may not be a threat to their lives. I know the power of emotional blackmail only too well. The manipulation can be so fierce that you yield for whatever reason. It is unfortunate but yes, even people as close as a spouse can be envious of you and try to control you. I know men who are threatened by their wives' beauty, charisma, strength, friendliness, and achievements and use all avenues to pull them down. You would have thought in the real world you would aspire to uphold something that you love. Women who are weak yield and make these men winners—at the expense of their own personal growth. Wake up and smell the rose ladies! Instead of enjoying, embracing, upholding and simply living life, one uses negative control. The downfall is the controller continues to have the same negative emotions of inadequacy, low self-esteem, and hopelessness forever. And to justify their act, they will not strive to reform.

Equally, some men use their achievements to put women in their lives under their feet. It is definitely not a comfortable position to be. When one is financially dependent on them, these freaky men walk all over their spouse or partner. The painful reality is that for anyone to place such control on you, it is entirely your fault. No one should allow another human being to control him or her no matter what. Anyone who treats another human being in such a manner has some form of mental illness. They may actually have some inadequacies that they are desperately trying hard to cover. It shouldn't really be like this, you cannot make yourself better by negatively inflicting your painful, bad character on others. A well-rounded human being does not feel the need to control or undermine another person in any shape or form. We need to accept our situations at any time in life. We should aspire to reach our aspirations from a motive within to be successful, not because your friend has this or the other that you do not have.

Not everyone has the same goals or can be as well achieved or established as the next person. We have to learn to either accept where we are or work towards where we want to be. I love the position of knowing where I want to be, no matter how long it may take to get there. For instance, I love to smell and touch the money that would give me the kind of life style I aspire to. So I would have to work on strategies of how to get there. Removing myself from people with negative energy and those who will not encourage my ambitions would be the starting point.

One of the greatest tools for coping with life is to stay positive amidst all obstacles. It may not be easy depending on your personality or the circumstances surrounding you, but you have to teach yourself as it is the only way out of misery. Some people like to be miserable, you might say, I do not believe anyone under the sun wants a life of misery. Some people just have it the wrong way. Thinking that by being miserable, other people will feel sorry for them and try to reach out to them. That must be the saddest way to live your life, and unless this people gain an insight into this problem, no help will be sought. Misery only alienates the very people you are trying to draw into your self-pity. The world is cruel; no one wants to be hanging about people who are constantly miserable no matter what you say to them.

Sometimes we may feel justified in feeling envious of someone's achievements especially when you know they are wicked. Remember, you have not created a human being, so it is not your place to envy them. The Bible states that the wicked prosper, but their prosperity is not based on inner peace. If someone prospers at the expense of others, can you really call that success? You do not have to be spiritual to know the answer to that. The key is that whatever measure you use to be envious of others, you are still the victim. If I choose bitterness towards my experiences in UK, I am indeed the victim.

Chapter Eighteen
The Real World

As people, we all have an interpretation of what the real world entails. Looking at the realities of life, its experiences and challenges, many of us may conclude that the world is not an ideal place to be. There is so much suffering. People die daily, some suffer from chronic illnesses or depression. There is cruelty to children; there are disasters in the form of tsunamis and hurricanes. The list can go on and on. What is ideal for one person may not be for the next.

The words of a preacher have stayed in my mind for years since listening to his sermon. His opening statement was "life does not care who you are." Had I not stayed throughout the sermon, I would have made a wrong conclusion of his intention and meaning. When I looked deeply into it, I realized that indeed anything can happen to anyone at any time regardless of whether you are rich or poor, kind or wicked, pray three times a day, give to the poor, and so on. This is the feeling I experienced when reading the book of Ecclesiastes in the Bible—when Solomon said life is useless. I thought about the wisdom God gave Solomon, how he enjoyed his life in its goodness and remained in favour of God. Solomon was the son of King David with his concubine Bathsheba. When you think about it, God looked beyond any human error and saw the need of the soul. I am not intending to suggest that we should make excuses for our wrongdoings just because God's grace covers us. Nonetheless, whatever is bound to come your way will come no matter what you do. This view, like one brother said, goes with the idea of predestination, a theory I do not believe as it would undermine the purpose of prayer. However, some things in life we will never really understand. You wonder how many good people have undeserved calamities? In my view and those who share it, God permits certain things to happen to humanity for a reason even though it might not be His will. You may think about situations where you permit your children against your will, certain choices they make which may end up in disaster. You gave them freedom of choice, but unfortunately the consequences were undesirable. Life is life. You just have to make the best out of it, let go, and let God's will be done.

When my children come running to me, crying about how another child has been unkind, I give them a hug, but go on to point out that life is not a smooth road. They will meet bumps and humps along the way, and they will have to learn how to deal with their friends.

Children are similar in their behaviour as they try to understand themselves regardless of their ethnic orientation. But living in England has made me weary of the added challenges my children and those in our situation face. As described throughout the book, the dynamics of living in a white-dominated society brings added challenges to children and adults. Children can be cruel due to lack of insight on the impact their behaviour has on another child. This is the reason we need balanced adults who can teach the children. When my daughter had a challenge of feeling isolated among her classmates, my heart crumbled! I feared for her, as I know she is a very soft-spoken, very kind, little girl with much love to share. I had to ask her specific questions about whether she thought this was based on the fact that she is different (in colour) from them, whether she thought they hated her. This is not exactly the kind of questions you want to be asking an eight-year-old child. But reality hits you and you have to act in the best interest of your child. You endeavour to protect your child as much as you can, but also you have to teach them to stand their ground. As a mother, this set me on a crumbling ground, one where I know deep down I have to fight for my children. The fear of them facing the isolation I have faced put me in a place where I never wanted to be, that is going deeper into colour-coded lives. This is reality whether we like it or not. You can only pray that your children will maintain their self-confidence and believe in themselves and not what the next person says, whether an adult or child.

As I said in earlier chapters, prejudice comes from a lack of knowledge or exposure and continues because society is still not educated. Some people choose to be prejudiced not so much from ignorance but because they are destined to live a life of misery. It must sure be disturbing to live with the burden of disliking others for being different. Children simply portray what they hear from their parents and the society of ignorant people who have low-class mentality. I can face my reality and vent my way through, but what about the children? Why has society come this far and placed people in boxes that only the strong can survive? A friend told me of her childhood experience as a minority growing up in what is rightfully her country and yet faced an intense sense of not belonging to the white world. She told of how she gave up developing any meaningful relationships with the white folk as it wouldn't be real. This does not mean that there aren't genuine people in the white society. My friends and acquaintances would wonder what I meant if I embraced such ideologies. But equally, they identify with the position I am in even though I believe they will never fully understand it. There is a Sesotho saying, "Seata se utloa ke mongasona ho opa," meaning "you are the only person who feels the pain of your circumstances."

This is still the world where "white dominance" rules people's lives whether we want to accept it or not. A world where you don't always get whatever it is you hoped for or dreamed it would be. I had a very different dream coming to the UK, and the reality is beyond any form of anticipation. Should you stop living? Definitely not, pressing on is the only way out. You have to keep striving to be the best you can be. A world where two wrongs do not make it right, so you have to be the better person.

This is the world where justice is not the order of the day. A world where conflict between appearance and reality coexists, where society fails to protect the innocent, the wicked go unpunished, and good people get a share of untoward calamities. It is survival of the fittest like in the jungle. A world where outward appearance is deceiving, people tend to pretend all is well instead of facing their reality. The real world is indeed the one I have awakened to, a world where poor upbringing does not make up for the later life. The same real world that questions the existence of God, the Maker of the universe, and yet the theories to prove His nonexistence are not substantial. In this world, those in power abuse it at the expense of others. The religious figures that most people look up to seem to be the worst with corruption. Unfortunately, many get put off of religion due to some of these realities, which is a shame, really. I guess that is why Jesus did not advocate for organized religion, as this is where good intentions turn into a bitter battlefield of indifference.

On a holiday to Dublin over one particular Easter break, we were passing by a Catholic church on Easter Sunday as people were going into morning mass. A couple of people were gathering around and there were police (Garda) on the side of the road watching. Two people were giving an account of how as children they were abused by the Catholic priests. They spoke of physical abuse, sexual abuse, emotional torture, and you name it. The woman made me cry when she expressed how full of hatred she was and that she will never forgive because of the damaging effects of her abuse. She had never seen her mother as she was taken away shortly after she was born, because the mother was not married. Who knows, they may have tortured her to death in the name of God. My heart went out to her, because she will continue carrying a life burdened by not forgiving and not believing in God. They had misrepresented God big time to her. I wished I could have a chance to say to her to forgive so as she can be set free. Not being able to forgive binds you, and haunts you, and unfortunately, it becomes your disease no matter how legitimate it is that you feel that way. Look at where the real world puts people. By the time we walked away from the scene, I felt sad for these people and many more who have faced similar torture in the name of religion.

In this world, no matter how good your intentions are they will be misinterpreted in one form or another, even by people you thought understood your motives. As I keep on walking and trying to understand relations between people, it would appear that no one really ever understands fully another person. And it may not be far-fetched that the behaviours of most white people towards non-white emanates from many years of ignorance or that they simply cannot be bothered by people outside their circle. For years, the media has taught a white superiority that will continue for years till a completely new culture is born. When white people went to Africa for instance, they went there to capture, colonize, and make their life easy. The immigrants coming to England come mostly for economic reasons, some as refugees, and some for studies. The society in return makes them unwelcome for fear of the unknown—it could be mostly racial.

As for the bigger picture, I would like to tell the world that regardless of how bold, strong, and friendly I appear, I have faced the isolation, prejudice, and stigmatization of being in a "white" world. And I have no room for hatred, as it would be a waste of space. I am just sad that this is the real world. My wish therefore is how can we all make it better? A lot of strong leaders have pioneered a move away from prejudice, but it lives on. How much education is required to remove these barriers of ignorance? I am without any doubt comfortable with myself, and I am not seeking attention in any form, but I would love a harmonious environment where stereotypes become a thing of the past. Keep dreaming, you might think!

What is the general message for all of us? For those of you under the bondage of crippling attitudes emanating from ignorance, it is time to wake up and smell the coffee. I call this bondage because it must be a sad place to be—ruled by prejudice. I have come across people who will tell you how racist they were till they opened their eyes to human reality. Often these people had no reason to hate someone of a different colour except that was all they knew. You can clearly see the damaging effects the society that propagated these attitudes has created. I wish I could talk to one person with racist hatred and that they could tell me where in the world this sort of burden sits in their heart and whether they are actually at peace with themselves. There cannot be true peace on such grounds. It's something I am not able to touch as to how feeling superior to someone makes you a better being. It can only enslave you, truly. Yes, we are different, let's leave it at that

To those of us in a "box" facing victimization due to racial prejudice, tell your stories, voice your concerns to colleagues, managers, leaders, etc. The truth is if we were all brave and told those who are racists on a closer, personal contact that they are racists, they would panic so much with the idea of you even mentioning it that it would leave no room for further discussion regardless of its truth. To the beneficiaries of a system that victimizes others, take a moment and reflect: are you biased of others just because of colour? What benefit are you gaining by being unfair to others? Is this not the same world that encourages justice?

I will keep on dreaming of the ideal world like most of us. Throughout this journey, I have developed a passion for teaching society about prejudice. I would love to start at the very beginning—the children. I would promote an idea of a fully developed curriculum in schools. In universities, we presently touch on issues of culture and diversity, but I believe it is not adequate. Britain has become one of the world's major countries as a multiracial society with diverse ethnicities and nationalities. This society needs to accept that these non-white people have built this country as well. The country would not survive without us. And yes, I love being in England as my journey continues.

In some of his writings on issues of race, Dr. Michael Eric Dyson depicts how one should love themselves despite whatever circumstance. He states that we should acknowledge things the white folk have done to harm the universe, but have no place to hate. Nelson Mandela set such an amazing precedent by choosing a peaceful approach to the people who threw him in jail for more than two decades. At the time of his release from prison there was a major move of the white Afrikaners mainly to the UK, fearing that Mandela would promote a system of revenge. What a great lesson to us all. The reality, though, still stands that it's not every white person who was inspired by such humility. Those with a plan to hate continue to hate even today. We can only aspire to move on to a better world of humanity, to one that has a different light. I want to be an agent of change in our world, because staying bitter and twisted is much bigger price. Super soul Sunday is one of the programmes I love watching presented by Oprah. She interviewed a Referent one time on issues of spirituality. I was intrigued by his comment when he stated that his role was to turn the human race into human family. I thought what great thinking-my sentiments exactly!

Food for thought: "Whatever is true, whatever is noble, whatever is right, whatever is pure, whatever is lovely, whatever is admirable-if anything is excellent or praise worthy-think about such things (Phillipians 4:8), one of my favourite Bible text. We have to strive to be better people, for a better community, in building a society that is diverse-"variety is the spice of life"!

Thank you for reading my book.

Bibliography

Brown, Keith M. *An Incredible Journey: From Religion to Liberation.* Milton Keynes: AuthorHouse UK Ltd., 2011.

Edmonds, Noel. *Positively Happy: Cosmic Ways to Change Your Life.* London: Ebury Publishing, 2006.

Holy Bible: The New International Version. London: Hodder & Stouhton, 2004

Garner, Lesley. *Everything I've Ever Learned About Love.* London: Hay House UK, 2005.

Lindenfield, Gael. *The Positive Woman.* London: Thorsons, 1992.

Khosi: Drum Magazine: *Do you remember your first hairstyles?* Drum Magazine Issue 1 Sring/Summer.South Africa..2012

Obama, Barack. *Dreams From My Father.* Edinburgh: Canongate Books Ltd., 2008.

Osteen, Joel. *Become a Better You: 7 Keys to Improving Your Life Every Day.* New York: Simon & Schuster Ltd., 2007.

Seete, Thembi: My hair Story: Drum Magazine Issue 1 Spring/summer. South Africa..2012

Sewel, Tony. *Keep on Moving: The Windrush Legacy-The Black Experience in Britain from 1948.* London: Voice Enterprises Ltd., 1998.

Timberlake, Lloyd. *Africa in Crisis: The Causes and Cures of Environmental Bankruptcy.* London: Earthscan Publications Ltd., 1988.